th

Safe Room

Carol Mog

Unity Publishers
A Division of Bridge-Logos
Alachua, Florida 32615 USA

Unity Publishers
A Division of Bridge-Logos
Alachua, FL 32614 USA

The Safe Room
by Carol Mog

Library of Congress Catalog Card Number: 2008922442
International Standard Book Number 978-1-93172-722-8

Scripture quotations in this book are from the *King James Version of the Bible.*

Acknowledgements

This book would not have been possible if not for the brave women who chose to share their stories. But, even more courageous was their determination to heal with God's help from a past that would have taken from them any joy of living.

Thanks go to those who have helped with the editing of this book and those who have been with me through the writing process. I know that I could not have done it without you.

Because Sage Pappas (Mason) graciously offered her condo for these women to meet; she provided a safe venue that allowed them to be there for one another and to learn more about God's love for them.

I hear many people acknowledging how much their husbands mean to them, but only God truly knows the magnitude of my thankfulness for my husband, Denny; a man who only has encouraged me, always standing by me.

And Carol Frances is always thankful to Katherine Anne.

Finally, I give all the glory to God. He is a God who heals and provides a way through in His Word.

Dedication

I dedicate this book to those who shared their stories.

Contents

CHAPTER 1

The Safe Room

When I think about all the young women in my Bible study group, I experience anew the fulfillment that comes when one is led by God and follows that lead.

About eleven years ago, I felt a real desire to start a Bible study group for young women that would emphasize how the Bible works for us rather than attempting to learn a lot of Biblical knowledge.

This idea came to me after a young woman who at the end of her counseling session said "I wish you had been my mother." I realized that I wished that her mother had been the mother a young child needed and is designed to have. So many present and former clients were like this one, they had never experienced being lovingly guided by a mother. They never had the safety they were supposed to have in childhood. Instead, they struggled with feelings of insecurity, fears of abandonment and rejection, anger issues, panic attacks and an underlying depressive state.

When God impressed upon my mind to begin this group, I immediately began to argue with Him. I was too busy, too tired, and had no time. But God persisted in calling me to this ministry. More clearly, I heard Him telling me that young women needed older women to mentor them so that they might become mentors or a "Naomi" for other young women someday. After struggling with God for about two months, I sent out invitations to a Bible study to as many young women as He put on my mind. I got a good response as well as one young woman offering her home, so the group began. To my delight, I am never tired on the every other Wednesday that the group meets, and have actually added a wonderful dimension to my life.

The women all had such good minds, quick wits, sensitive hearts and excellent abilities, but emotional instability prevented them from functioning in life as they needed to do. Their response to someone who genuinely cared for them was all the reward anyone would want. Yet sadly, they could not respond nearly as well to boyfriends, husbands, parents or even their biological children at times. It became clear that in their minds these significant others are supposed to be there for them, which put these young women right back in that place where the child wanted the parent to love them and meet their needs.

Having experienced a childhood that lacked the needed components of love, safety and significance, I had learned that the only one who could meet that need for me was God. Many wonderful people are a part of my life but I do not expect them to fill the void that poor parenting and abuse left. At an early age I experienced God filling that void, and He has continued to do so for fifty-seven years. Maybe, as God helps me to mentor these young women, they will learn and experience that safety in God.

The women in this group do not all go to church on a regular basis, and many are just beginning to believe in a God who wants to get involved in our lives. But, they have become very closely knit. They have learned a great deal about themselves and about each other. And they have indeed learned how well the precepts of the Bible work. These women are all unique, yet, they seem to have a common thread. Perhaps, that common thread is the need to feel loved and significant in life

Most of the women work outside of the home. Some are married, divorced, widowed, single, or remarried. They certainly know the meaning of suffering; they are all are survivors. Most are still overcoming. When these women are together they seem to embrace one another. Maybe a better way of saying this is, through their time together they have found the wonderful sense of fulfillment that comes from being there for one another.

Somehow, being able to make such a positive difference strengthens the child who feels so unsafe within, hidden behind an adult who is somewhat superficial or at best one-dimensional in her presentation of the total person. Sometimes this adult is a high performance person, a very social person, one who makes everyone else laugh or perhaps one who wants to take care of everyone. The women have come to realize, mostly from the Bible and from discovering and sharing themselves with each other, that perfection is an illusion. That God really works best through our weaknesses. It is His perfection that we strive to walk in.

As we worked together to learn how the Bible works for us and understand how God keeps children through very difficult times, we could see many things more clearly. We discovered that the coping mechanisms we used as children to survive various types of abuse, are the ones we continue to use in our adult lives when we are overwhelmed. It is simply a learned behavior.

We began identifying these various coping mechanisms, or fragments of our personality, as young children. Even though we fragmented for different reasons, we learned that the coping mechanisms each of us used were almost the same. When you watch little children on the playground, you can often watch some of these fragments being developed. For instance, when a child is not socially accepted by others, he may act as though he doesn't care. Or, he may try to get them to like him by giving them things or being very nice. Yet, again, he may become the class clown and try to make them laugh hoping to find acceptance. As the child grows older, especially if his home environment is negative, he might have a very humorous fragment for which he is known, or one that looks out for everyone, or one that tends to avoid social interaction.

In my experience, most people who are survivors of a difficult childhood tend to have many of these fragments, but usually one or two are stronger than the others.

One Sunday afternoon one of the young women of the group showed up at my front door with a plastic grocery bag filled with all of her diaries. She handed them to me and said, "This is me; if I give them to you, maybe it will help." This wonderful person is married and the mother of two children; she struggles with substance abuse (alcohol). I am not concerned that it is a chemical addiction so much as it being her only escape from the pain and hurt she feels. The first time she came to see me was on a Thanksgiving Eve, and she had been drinking. She was unable to stay in one presentation—she went from crying to being angry, then became fearful. Her fragments were very apparent when she was out of control, whether it was from alcohol or something else that was just too much for her to handle.

I began reading her journals and found that I was accurate about the severe fragmentation. All the fragments that usually present themselves in one's life, when one is repressing something, were there. As I read, I found a very sad, lonely, little girl. She wanted to be loved. Yet, along with her was the little girl who could not make anyone be there for her, so she decided that there would never be anyone who would love her. In the journal she actually said over and over, "I am so lonely; if only I had someone to love me." She then talked about how she thought she had finally found someone to take away her lonely feelings, but it was not the one she was dating. When she finally won the heart of the new man she felt would take away her loneliness, she began to feel as though she had made a terrible mistake and constantly wrote about the possibility of getting back with her former boyfriend. The child who was longing for love always continued to search for it. Right beside her, sabotaging her efforts, was the one who said no one was ever going to love her.

Also quite obvious was the little child who was very afraid. She didn't seem to know why, but she could not stand to be alone. As I continued reading this person's life through her journals, I was humbled by the unbelievable privilege of having this young woman trust me with all of her. Often, in the journals I read that she felt she did not make any sense; she could not understand herself, so how could she expect anyone else to? Several times she wrote that she wondered if she could ever really let anyone read her journals.

At a very early age, these youngsters who are hurting develop a part that I refer to as the "performer." They just keep busy and block everything out of their minds. How often do we in our adult lives say that we just have to get busy and put that out of our minds? When a child develops this performer fragment at an early age, their performer usually far exceeds the average capability of the average person. The reason for this is that the child's entire mind is devoted to this task. The performer is one-dimensional.

An example of this concentration is seen in professional sports. I have often heard NBA players say that when at the free-throw line, they have learned how to separate the 'shooter' from the emotional parts of their personalities. They are not in tune to anything but the rim, the crowd noise or their own emotions have no input. Blocking out everything but putting that ball through the rim is essential to being a good free-thrower. It is easy to see that the horrible abuse that many children suffer is much more important to escape than that of screaming crowds or fear of a missed free throw.

This seems to be a good spot to mention that those people who have experienced safety in early childhood often find that a survivor of a difficult childhood may come across as rather shallow and self-seeking or controlling. It is not unusual to have significant others say they just don't understand the person; she is so moody. In the group we have learned to understand this, respect it, and accept it. Only then are we able to present to God all of ourselves to receive His love and protection.

Continuing with the personality fragments that were in the journal, we find the one who always wants to *run away*. This part of a survivor's personality deals with *if only*. Running away can be seen in many ways: running away to go shopping, eating, not eating, driving around in a car for hours, leaving a marriage, changing careers, etc. This part of one's personality can cause a lot of trouble for other fragments, especially the performing one. My client presented this part of herself often in the journal. She went back to school three times to get a degree and on each occasion ran from it. She had too many things on her plate while trying to go to school. Because each activity was intended to meet the need of one of the fragments, whether it was the social fragment or the performer, she tried to do them all.

Another fragment of this client wanted to curl up in a ball and hide. Some of the girls in the group talked about the times when all they seem to want to do is stay in bed. In bed and under the covers is often a safe place for a child to hide, even in the daytime.

The list of fragments goes on; there is the one who is very witty. I refer to this as the "humorous" part. She is very funny and can make everyone laugh, and actually sometimes does not know when to stop. In this client's case she was having trouble dealing with the conflicting parts of herself, the one who is sexual and the part that hates sex. The "sexy" one was always there when she wanted to win a man's attention, but after she was going out with him and even more so after marriage, she had to deal with that part of her that did not like sex at all. The women in the group could certainly relate to that and admitted that their husbands were not too happy about it. The husbands just never seemed to understand it.

As my client's journal demonstrates, one of the most difficult things to handle, as all the women will attest to, is the arguing that goes on inside her head. In this particular person's case, when she cannot keep busy, make someone laugh or do something risky, (oh yes, we must not forget the "risk-taker," the one who denies the very frightened part of herself,) and has only the arguing inside her head, she will start to get in touch with the frightened and sad parts of herself and will turn to alcohol as a way of escape.

Often I am asked why you cannot just go forth in Christ. How can you go forth when you have big emotional chains holding you in the past and determining your behavior, which is dysfunctional at best? In Psalm 51:6, we are told that God wants truth in the innermost parts. If we can allow the Holy Spirit to light up these things for us, we are then and only then able to release them unto God. You cannot walk away from what you don't know.

For many years of my life, including the early years of my marriage, I was very afraid of being alone. Often when my husband Denny was at a meeting late in the evening, I would hear noises, and in my mind they would become the very worst things possible. Often, I would just lie almost paralyzed in bed hoping for my husband's quick return. When Denny got home, I would have him listen to the noise. He would investigate and find its origin and relieve my fears by explaining it to me. When, again, he was gone and I heard the same noise, I would not like it, but, I would remember its origin and not be so frightened. I believe it is the same with repressed memories or emotions. Whenever life becomes overwhelming we begin to feel those emotions and begin to try everything at our disposal to get away from the feelings. Once we have learned what happened in our lives to cause these feelings, we are less and less afraid. We have learned what it is that "goes bump in the night."

The group members have dealt with many questions: "Why is it that Christians are so reluctant to give all of themselves to God?" "Why are our churches filled with unhealed people?" "Why can't church be like our group meetings?" They do not grow at church and most of the time they do not find solace there.

Self-rejection is the thing that I feel plagues most of us in the Christian community. At each meeting I watched these precious women constantly reject themselves. They hated their fears, anger, sadness and often their inability to cope with life.

We were able, through working together, to see that the only way the child could survive was to forget or reject the wounded child. They believed that they just had to grow up, be successful, find someone to love them, have children, and be happy. It didn't seem to be working. They even turned to God and found they couldn't be contented Christians. From the sermons they heard and from the teachings that were shared in the various Christian classes they attended, they began to believe that if you became a Christian then everything in your life should be wonderful, so they presented to God their "performer" or their "people-pleaser" or the one who "wants everyone to love her." They try very hard to keep the "angry one" the "fearful one" the "sad one" etc. out of sight.

I was not raised in a religious home. When I use "religious" in this case I am referring to a home where we are taught that we need to be a certain way for God to love us. Most of the time this message is not overtly given, but I have learned that many children feel this way. This will be addressed in a broader sense throughout this book.

When I felt the call of God on my life at the age of twelve, it was after trying to take my life at eleven and a half and then deciding to become a cruel person and get even with all who had hurt me, I was on my way to create a 'mean' me, because she wouldn't hurt so much, and she would be afraid of no one. And, most importantly, she would never cry again. It would no longer make any difference to her that no one loved her or seemed to want her. Part of my program towards creating the mean fragment was to go to a little church around the corner from my house and make fun of the congregants. This small church started in a tent and now was in a basement. I remember well, kneeling outside the window in the grass and watching the people inside. They clapped their hands, raised their arms to God, sang and prayed very loudly. I began to laugh at them, whilst inside I yearned to be one of those kids sitting beside her parents in that church.

As I walked home that night, I found that tears were rolling down my face, and I was furious. But I could not rid myself of the longing for the love and joy I saw in those people's faces as I made fun of them. So, I continued to visit that small church and actually went inside and sat in one of the last pews, and a couple of months after my initial visit, I asked Christ into my life. I longed for and received not only His love but His friendship, His companionship. I asked Him to allow me to love as He did. I gave to Him what I really felt about myself. I held nothing back. To Him I gave the part that believed she was unlovable, and He loved her. I gave the frightened part, and He held her close. I felt no need to hide these things from God. You see, I was still a child, and in my childlike innocence, I wanted Jesus for all of me. As adults, we have already built walls of protection around ourselves and have invalid beliefs that often keep us from this intimacy with God. As I had no need to hide anything from God, I did not repress anything. Thus, there were no awful noises that I did not recognize. It sounds so simple doesn't it? That's exactly what Jesus wanted it to be, and that is why He says we must become as children. Only He can give to the child within, what it was intended by its Creator to have: love, safety and significance.

CHAPTER 2

Counseling Technique

This seems to be a good juncture to talk about a counseling technique that God gave to me. I call it "The Safe Room."

One day when I was working with people and feeling their discomfort when they talked about themselves, God brought to my mind all the safe ways Christ showed His disciples and followers a better way to understand themselves. He used parables, miracles, revelations that only God would know, and He made himself vulnerable and known to them. They saw His tears when Lazarus died and His anger that the money changers in the temple were robbing people. I began to think of the factor of safety for my clients and how important it is. As I was pretty well aware of God's enabling me to show love and acceptance to my clients, an idea came to me (I believe from God) of an exercise that would help my clients to get in touch with themselves. I call this exercise "The Safe Room," which is the title of this book and a technique that I have been able to share with other counselors who have found it very helpful in their practices.

It is usually apparent to me when a client is ready for the Safe Room. Sometimes, I can do it with her on her first visit;

for others, it takes longer. I ask them to lie down and I begin. The exercise goes like this:

"Allow your body to fall into the sofa. Beginning with your head and going all the way to your feet, feel yourself relaxing into the sofa. Now, listen to what I say and visualize the scene with me.

Picture a very large rectangular room. The most important thing I want you to remember is that this is a safe room; nothing or no one can hurt you there. It is protected by angels. At one end of our large room is a very big window with a window seat. As we look out of our window, we see a path sloping gently downhill lined on either side with trees. It is the peak of autumn. The leaves on the trees are bright yellow, orange and red. If we watch closely, we can see some leaves floating to the path below.

If we look above the trees, we see a perfectly blue sky; there are no clouds. The sun is splashing into our safe room through the window. On one of the long walls there is a fireplace with a low-grade fire in it. It is a chilly day, and we want our room to be warm.

About in the center of the room is a small, decorative, cheery table. In the center of the table is a big vase filled with beautiful flowers of vivid colors. The flowers seem to be cascading out of the vase. If we look at the top of the table, we can see the reflection of the vase and flowers. You can paint the room any color you would like, or you can wallpaper it.

It can have wall-to-wall carpeting, hardwood floors with or without area rugs. Whatever you would like. All around the room are comfortable chairs and couches.

I want you to watch as all the parts of your personality come into the room and find a place they want to go. I want to talk about some of the parts of my personality to give you an idea of what I am looking for. (Sometimes this is not necessary, the clients just begin to talk about what they see.) There is a part of my personality that is easily afraid. She is only three years old and she is lying across a big wing- back chair, and she is completely covered by a blanket. She really believes that if she can't see anything, no one can know that she is there. I have another part of my personality that is easily frustrated, she can cry when she is angry. She is nine years old and is pacing back and forth in the room. She is angry with her stepfather and wants to kill him but she is also very afraid of him. And, there is another part of myself who only wants to be like Jesus, and she is kneeling in front of a sofa. Now, take a few minutes and when you see someone or something, tell me about it."

People who have repressed memories or emotions almost immediately feel as if they are in the room. It becomes a very real experience and sometimes frightens them, because they do get in touch with how they feel. As we progress into the book some of the women will share parts of themselves that are in the room and why they are there. Briefly I will share other clients' experiences in the safe room. I want to share as clearly as possible with you how little children cope.

CHAPTER 3

Hiding

What do little children do with things that hurt or frighten them? They need to get them out of sight, out of their minds. They hide them. It is interesting to note that children hide things in the places where they see their parents hide things.

Some favorite hiding places of the clients I have seen are closets, especially on the top shelf where children cannot reach. Boxes are wonderful for hiding things. Kids then store the boxes in all the right places like the attic, the basement, or the garage. One child said all her memories are wrapped in freezer wrap and are in the freezer (this child's mother did a lot of freezing and canning). For another little boy a filing cabinet was the perfect place to put his secrets and then he locked it up. One little girl, about whom we will talk later, took all the bad things that happened to her and put them in her head when she was eleven years old and then took her head off. A favorite thing for children to do is to tell the secrets to their pets, dolls, or stuffed animals, because they will never tell anyone.

Now, I think it is pretty obvious where children got these ideas. I remember saying to my children, "Quick, company's coming. Throw these in the closet, out of the way." The young boy who hid things in a filing cabinet had a father who was a teacher or pastor and who always had a filing cabinet around.

Can't you see the little boy watching his father taking the papers he has been working on, filing them in the cabinet and then locking the drawer? I am sure the boy may have heard from his dad that the cabinet was a place he could put important things and know they were always there. No one could get to those important papers without the key.

In addition we know how often parents store things in the attic and basement. These are places to put things out of view. Often we run across something we have stored years ago and have completely forgotten that we ever had it.

I loved the little girl who put everything bad that had happened to her in her head and then took off her head. I asked the young woman if she remembered anything her mother might have said that gave her that idea. She said she was always saying, "What's wrong with you? You act like you have no head on your shoulders."

From working with clients, I have learned that children who could not find solace from their parents or caregivers often formed a strong alliance with animals, both real and stuffed. Animals just want to love us and have us love them back. They can't talk, so they can never tell anyone the secrets the child has told them. It is so good to have someone with whom scary things can be shared.

Another wonderful thing that children do is to hide themselves. One little boy would hide himself in the middle of a dark closet whenever he heard loud screaming. (This adult male came to see me because his wife found him sitting in the closet in the dark.) Children also make themselves disappear. If they are not there, no one can hurt them. One little girl would turn herself into a sheet of paper and slide under the couch cushion. Children who are being beaten or hurt badly can go into the wall or even into furniture, as one child did.

Of course, all of this is a means of dissociating. My clients who have endured severe trauma in their lives, and have always repressed it, have a part of themselves that watches them. They tell me that they often feel as though they are on the outside looking in.

Secret compartments; in beds, in closets
Behind something
In silence
In reading
In humor
In anger

Children can always find a place to hide themselves or their secrets.

CHAPTER 4

Laurie

The sun filtered through lacy curtains making funny shadows on the floor. Laurie tired quickly of pretending they were playing tag with her.

"Mommy, Mommy, please play with me," Laurie said as she tugged on her mother's skirt. Her mother was drying the dishes she had just washed and was keeping an eye on the coffeepot on the stove. "No, Laurie, Mommy is busy now and I have to get supper started. Why don't you go play with your brother?"

Laurie turned away, her bottom lip sticking out in front of her chin. She knew Freddie didn't want to play with her, he told her so. Just as she was leaving the room there was a knock at the side door. Laurie almost tripped as she ran to the door, jumping to look through the glass to see who it was. "Maybe it's Suzie," she said. The door opened and a man's head peeked in. "Hello. Anybody home?"

"Oh, it's only Ron from next door." Laurie said as she dragged her feet and started to walk away, mumbling as she went, "Nobody to play with."

"Well now, thank you for that warm welcome," Ron said as he tapped Laurie on the shoulder. Laurie could tell that her mother was upset so she said she was sorry. Then Laurie just *stood there, in her pink dress, staring at the floor and pushing the toe of her shoe into the floor.*

"Nobody to play with? What about me?" Ron said. "That is if you don't mind playing with a grumpy grown-up and if your mother doesn't mind." Laurie giggled and her mother laughed at the funny face and silly voice Ron made, as he said, "The mailman left these packages at the house by mistake. I'll leave them here on the table and then we'll get out of Mommy's way. OK?"

"OK," shouted Laurie as she ran out of the kitchen. Mommy just shook her head and smiled. Ron was so good with children. She was soon busy with her supper preparations and didn't notice the passing time after Ron and Laurie went to play. Neither did she notice that Laurie had run up the stairs and into her room. She offered Ron a cup of coffee when he walked into the kitchen and asked "Had enough of little-girl games?" Ron laughed, said he had to get home to his own supper and then left.

Upstairs Laurie sat on the floor talking to her dolls. They all seemed very impressed when she said her playmate that day had been a grown-up. "We played tag and hide-and-go-seek and had so much fun. He even said he had new games we could play another time; but that part's a secret. See, only special girls get to play those games." By now Laurie was dancing and spinning around the room, her skirts floating with the motion. She landed on her bed, all smiles and feeling good. "I'm special," she said again as she joined the doll party she'd left earlier.

Laurie's parents were very good friends with Ron and his wife, Grace. They played cards and made homemade pizza and laughed a lot. Laurie enjoyed the visits too, although they were often past her bedtime and she wasn't allowed to stay up. There were those special times, however, when Ron came over just to see "His best girl, Laurie." She felt so important.

This was no special day. Nothing out of the ordinary, but Laurie would never forget it because this was the day the games changed. Ron had been coming to play with her often, but now Ron was almost always "It" in tag; only he didn't tag her *anymore. He'd hold her tightly and tickle her. At first Laurie laughed and wiggled free to run again. Sometimes he held her so tightly she couldn't wiggle free and his tickles were hard. They hurt. That first day she finally broke free and instead of running to play again, she ran upstairs to her bedroom. When she sat on her bed, she was out of breath. Something had gone wrong but she wasn't sure just what. Laurie was troubled about it but felt better after she talked it over with her dolls. "Shh, it's a secret!" With that declaration made, she began a new tea party and all uneasiness was forgotten; for a while.*

Ron came to play again. This time he carried her down the stairs to the basement. Laurie sometimes wondered if it was okay with her mommy but since her mommy never said no to Ron, it must be okay. They were friends.

The games began to change and Laurie didn't like them. Ron touched her a lot in a lot of places. She didn't want to play with Ron any more. But he told her he was the grown-up, and he was good friends with her mommy and daddy, and he would tell them that she was very bad if she told them anything about their games. He said they would believe him and not her. He told her that bad things happen to little girls who can't keep secrets. He said all this and more without raising his voice, although his tone changed from friendly to sinister and his light hand on her shoulder turned into a strong grip.

He let her go then, and instead of running, she slowly walked up the stairs carrying a burden too great for her four years. She dragged her feet and Mommy scolded her for scuffing the toes of her shoes. Her heart sank. He was right, bad things do happen when you even think about telling secrets.

So, Laurie kept their secret and her pain deep inside. Ron didn't come very often, but when he did, her body went limp, her eyes went blank, and she felt no joy. (Laurie's experience reveals that a child can somehow realize that such games are not appropriate. These games violated her innocence. Though he never penetrated her sexually, he penetrated her soul, nonetheless.) *The touching made her feel dirty and bad about herself. Then he wanted her to see him in a new way. One day he showed her something and wanted her to touch it. She knew boys were different from girls, that they go to the bathroom differently, but she never saw anything like this. Laurie shrank back but a firm hand held her. She saw the other parts too and was afraid. The grip increased till it hurt and the voice became a harsh whisper, "Remember about secrets and bad girls." Her heart raced; she had no choice but to touch it and then ducked under his grip and ran up the basement stairs. She caught his eye, as she glanced back to see if he'd chase her, but he only smiled in a way that made her sick. Talking to her dolls didn't help much anymore, so she became angry with them and refused their invitation to a tea party.*

Not too long after this, Laurie and her family moved to another state and life moved on; except for Laurie. Something inside her was stuck. Without realizing what was happening, Laurie's mind began to wall off the painful memories. Before too long she didn't even remember them anymore.

One might think –case closed, end of story, but it was only the beginning of life with a damaged heart. It didn't matter that the conscious memories were gone; Laurie had to live with the damage they held. You see, little girls are not just sugar and spice and everything nice. They are vulnerable creatures who wear their hearts on the outside. They're trusting, giving, loving and easily bruised. Growing up with a damaged heart has far-reaching implications. Laurie hated her own body and felt very ugly and out of place. She always tried to be good—at everything.

After a time, she couldn't allow herself to fail, not if she wanted to feel good about herself. All of her feelings about herself were determined by what she perceived others were thinking. She never felt good enough or smart enough or pretty enough or anything enough. Laurie would never stand up for herself. As a result, people could hurt her again, and she wouldn't tattle because "good girls" kept secrets. Another man, the father of a friend, touched her inappropriately when she slept. At first he just looked but then he sat on the bed and felt her private parts. She probably would have believed it to be a dream because she never fully awoke during the episode. However, he sealed her silence the next morning by saying that she said very bad things in her sleep that night. His facial expression and tone of voice made her feel dirty and bad. She couldn't tell anyone so the hurt was pushed deeper inside and another wall was built in her mind.

A stranger in a public place once approached Laurie from behind and inappropriately touched her. Laurie froze. A storm of confusion flooded her mind. It took every ounce of strength to break away. No one had held her; it was her fear.

I have learned through my counseling that children who are sexually abused often lose a sense of control. They often make up a part of themselves to handle this for them. When a perpetrator approaches them, this part takes over, allowing the abuse. This is especially true in cases of extreme sexual abuse at a very early age.

Wall-building was now a common, automatic process in Laurie's mind. By the time she was an adult, there were so many walls that she had few memories of who she was as a child and little room to learn who she was as an adult.

Mental walls have a way of crumbling here and there. When the mind can no longer keep up with the repairs, the person may break down emotionally. She may even seek help, but until she realizes the depth of the wounds, healing can't begin. Just as there were many walls, so there are many layers to be healed in her heart and mind.

It is possible. There is hope, with God's help for healing. But it is painful and takes time. Grown-up Laurie has to embrace the child Laurie and relive her pain so she can be whole. She can't reject her because in doing so, she is rejecting herself.

Meeting Laurie

Laurie and I once taught at the same school.

If you were to go by first impressions, Laurie appeared to be very self-contained and confident. Her abilities were well known, and I soon learned that she intimidated others. She was definitely introverted, and I was not. So, I decided to get to know her. She remained at that school after I left to become a full-time counselor. We had formed a friendship and continued to get together whenever possible.

Laurie always had physical problems. She had many allergies, which resulted in a lot of stomach problems. Her back was often out of alignment. More important, something that most people did not know, Laurie had lost complete function of her lower intestine. After going to many doctors, she was accepted in the research program of a major hospital. She tried all their new medicines and the general consensus of the doctors was that nothing could be done for this condition.

The years passed. More and more, Laurie suffered from depression and panic attacks, not having any idea of their origin. Her depression reached the point where she needed to take a leave of absence from her employment. At this time, Laurie asked me to give her professional counseling. This was the beginning of a long and arduous untangling of knotted-up fears and pain. It was not an easy thing for Laurie, but it was worth it to know herself and learn to identify and release the pain and fear.

Laurie could easily share memories of the volatile home situation in which she had been raised. Her parents were not Christians when she was little. Her father was always very angry and often directed his rage at Laurie's mother and two brothers. But Laurie was not the target of that rage. She felt it was her job to keep everyone calm. Once, a display of anger caused eight-year old Laurie to run from the house. Her father came after her begging her not to be upset. She knew how hard his job was, he said. He needed her not to be angry with him.

Laurie felt she was stuck in between her parents. This made her angry with her mom. She wanted her mom not to argue back—not to feed the father's rage. Blocking out emotions for either parent—setting herself away from them was the only place for Laurie. This enabled her not to react to them and neither one of her parents got upset with her. Often she felt that her siblings did not like her because dad never got upset with her.

Now, consider Laurie as she strives to exist in this environment, all the time hiding and fearing that men would again do terrible things to her.

In order to survive, Laurie fragmented into different coping mechanisms. Following is Laurie's narrative describing what she found when we did the Safe Room technique in therapy.

"The Room"

The ease of identifying the parts of myself as they appeare in the room surprises me. Upon entering the room it is as if things begin to appear out of the darkness. The bare essentials of the room emerge first. To the left there is a locked door and beyond that a window seat, just the right size for someone to curl up in and feel safe. Behind me, as I look around there is a teacher's desk with a desk lamp that shines light onto the desktop but not up into the room. There is a pretty sofa and two wing-back chairs. The corners of the room are dark. I am not sure but I think there is a window on the far wall behind heavy drapes.

Laurie did not allow herself to see all of the room. People and objects were shrouded in darkness. The first time that I took Laurie into the safe room, she saw only darkness but experienced a great deal of anxiety. She was not ready to see anything but could not avoid the emotions. When Laurie did begin to see the room, she did not allow herself to see a big room. In the Safe Room Technique, I ask clients to envision a very large, rectangular room. Laurie preferred small spaces as many clients do at first. As they get more in tune with themselves and their methods of coping, the room becomes much bigger. The locked door in this client's case referenced secrets. Often when I ask why clients have so little furniture or none at all, they reply: "If there is furniture, bad people can hide behind things." Laurie had some furniture, almost like a little sitting area with all the corners of the room darkened. Laurie indicated that she was in the room and could see a teacher's desk behind her. At this time Laurie was teaching so it made sense to me that she would encounter the teacher's desk.

The first part of myself to appear is a little girl about three years old. She is blonde and wears a frilly pink dress. She is all innocence; there is no sadness or pain associated with her. She is in the room but almost separate, untouched by the turmoil I feel. Lately, she has grown to become a young woman in her early twenties. Many times now she keeps switching back and forth from one to the other, but she is always on the window seat.

Behind the one chair is a little girl, about seven years old I think, who is hiding. She is a tomboy and playfully darts from one place to another, always semi-hiding. She wants to play and have fun but she has to hide too.

Curled up on the floor behind the other chair is another little girl. I can't remember her age, maybe five years old. She presents a stark contrast to the playful one just mentioned. This girl is lying in the fetal position for protection. She never looks up or uncurls. All of her pain is turned innermost where no one can touch it or her. She is "profound sadness."

Walking back and forth on the right side of the room, but not really pacing, is the singer. She is softness personified. Her hair and her bearing speak peace. She is feminine, wears a dress and never interacts with others. In fact, she is often absent from the room. Since the early visits to the room I have not seen her.

Leaning against the wall is the non-emotional one. She is not feminine looking at all. She wears slacks and leans on the wall with her arms crossed on her chest. She does not speak but communicates with her hands or facial expressions. She is a young adult.

Seated on the sofa is a young woman who is emotionally distraught, crying and physically shaking. The absence of peace, she is all anxiety and fear. Everything is frightening to her.

Outside the door stands "anger." She bangs on the door but it is locked and the others do not want her in the room.

The teacher is not seen much, in fact, I'm not sure I have seen her here. She is sad, depressed and defeated, without hope.

I think someone is in the dark corner in the back left of the room but it is only a guess.

Up above and to the right side of the room is the observer. There is no body to be seen just an observing presence. She enables me to look down on the scenes below.

There is a hallway that appears to the right, almost next to the non-emotional one. It only appears when Carol (she is referring to me) opens the door; otherwise there is a fireplace there. There is one part I met in the hallway but have never seen in the room. She is an ugly old hag about the height of the three-year-old. At first glance she would remind you of Cousin It on the Addams Family show except that she is black as soot, so very dirty. She is repulsive; no one would ever want to touch her. Actually, she is protecting the little girl in the pink dress. If she is repulsive then no one will want to hurt her so she has to believe that she is ugly and dirty. Protection. At one point I think Carol asked me to touch her. This took some effort but I was surprised when she immediately turned into the little girl in the pink dress. She protects the innocence of the child.

Lately two new additions have appeared. Seated in the chair near the sofa is a woman about thirty to forty years old. She is always frozen in one position—trying to reach out to the crying one on the sofa. She has short brown hair, a little curly. She is feminine and confident and wants to bring the parts together. She is what is hoped to be.

The last one to appear is "bad." That is her essence. Someone had to be bad so she carries it all. She truly believes she is bad. She is now a constant companion, standing to my left. I can feel her there as she is always speaking into my left ear. I don't think she is as tall as I am.

Although these are all the parts of me they do not share the same knowledge. Each one holds some part of it. Trying to find out who holds what secret or information is hard work and is often impossible. Even as I write now I can feel "anger" trying to break in. She does not like being restrained and silenced.

These parts of me are not totally separate entities or personalities but are shades of me. They are all always there, however some may be more apparent than others at any given moment.

There are many times when the room goes in and out of the darkness of my fear. My mind even wrecked the room for a few days to keep us from exploring further—but it cannot resist Carol's probing.

In the above narrative Laurie covers several sessions. After she envisioned the room, I asked her to just watch, to keep focused on the room. Then I asked for all the parts of Laurie to come into the room. That is usually all that I need to say. The first time we did this, Laurie saw the three-year-old, in a pink dress. As we uncovered more of the trauma of Laurie's past, the three-year-old became free to grow. (This explains why Laurie's narrative discusses how she grows older.) The sweetness and innocence of the three-year-old were things that Laurie rarely experienced. She mostly dealt with feelings of being ugly and dirty.

After two or three sessions, we met the seven-year-old who felt a need to hide but who wanted to play and have fun. In contrast, there is the five-year-old who was curled in the fetal position hoping to protect herself. In Laurie's story we learned that the parents' good friend sexually abused Laurie. This was done between the ages of three and six (her parents moved from that town when Laurie was six years old). It takes a child about two years to repress a memory after the last incidence of abuse.

The seven-year-old who wanted to play and put ugly things out of her mind was helping Laurie to forget.

As well as being a teacher, Laurie also sings professionally. No matter how bad she feels, how distraught, if she has a singing engagement that day, she will give a flawless performance. The "singer" does not allow any other part of Laurie to distract her from her singing. Laurie began singing in plays and even operas at a very young age. Again, the 'singer' helps Laurie put ugly thoughts out of her mind.

Everyone who has suffered severe childhood trauma has a non-emotional aspect to his personality. I think this can be true of almost all of us at particular times—those times when we feel overwhelmed but have obligations that must be met. We can focus on what we need to do and not feel the turmoil. But those who have had severe trauma go into this mode automatically. It is a very restful place for them to be, but they also talk to me about not being able to feel love for their husbands, children or even God when they are in this mode. I have heard many a child say, "I don't care if you don't want to play with me; it doesn't bother me." The child is attempting not to feel the hurt of being rejected. If childhood trauma is great enough and lasts long enough, the child will have had time to create a part of herself that does not feel.

The young woman sitting on the sofa in Laurie's narrative was her depressed part. It is important that we are in tune to this fragment, because she often talks about wanting to run her car into a tree. She is the one who will benefit from an antidepressant. At the same time, it is quite common among those who have dissociated to have a very happy part, who would never complain of depression. Also, many people have been depressed from childhood; they don't know that what they are feeling is not normal.

Laurie talks about "anger" being outside the room and trying to get in. More often than not when "anger" is in the room, the frightened children will not enter, as they are afraid of her. Anger can make a child feel stronger, and anger can also protect the child. If the child begins to feel very weak or afraid, if the Performer or none of the other modes can get her out of this mode, then "anger" comes in. Anger keeps others away from the child and later the adult, when she is feeling overwhelmed, so that she will not crumble. The child cannot crumble because someone may ask her what the problem is; she cannot reveal the problem or she will be hurt by the perpetrator or rejected by the parent. As an adult, crumbling may mean an inability to regain one's strength, so much has been held inside that if it all came out, it would seem impossible to regroup. A large part of the counseling process is to understand why a part was formed, its usefulness, and how even though the child needed it, it causes harm for the adult. I tell my clients not to think of getting rid of a part of themselves but rather to think of giving that part a new job description.

In her narrative Laurie shares how she has created another part of herself—one who reaches out to the depressed woman and wants to help. This is progress.

Sadly, as Laurie explains, there is a part of her that is "bad." How else can a child make any sense out of so much abuse in her life? It must be her fault—so often the client has a core belief that she is bad and not worth anyone's love. Often the perpetrator tells her that people will think she is bad if she tells their secret.

This is a good place to mention that once the "child" parts come into the room, I take one of them by the hand and suggest that there is a hallway before them with doors. If the child is afraid, I say that behind the doors are those things that frightened the child. I ask them how many doors there are. An angel accompanies us as we open each door and look at what is behind it. This is a very difficult part of the therapy for most. But, I have watched as grown men and women sigh in relief as we take the small children from the place that is frightening them and carry them into the safe room.

Laurie did not put in her narrative that she has a child part that can write mirror-image. Often her journal entries are done that way; a child believes that no one can know what she is writing.

Since the writing of that narrative, Laurie has made much progress in her healing. She often shares her experiences with groups of women in the hope that her journey may encourage them in some way. She also expresses her journey through writing. Below is a parable that she wrote.

"The Parable of the Trees"

I found myself walking in a valley of trees. Some had leaves that nearly danced in the breeze while others raised limbs in seeming praise and thankfulness. Some trees were tall, some short. Others were fat—or stout and some willowy. They grew in a lush field where the sun shone, the breeze blew, the rain fell and God's blessings were all around.

As I walked among the trees I noticed that some branches were heavy with fruit. Some looked a little battered but there was strength there too—holding on by faith, trusting that the rain would satisfy their thirst and that the sun would shine upon them, once again casting playful shadows with their leaves.

Wandering among the trees I saw some with brick walls built up around them, thick, tall, impenetrable walls. Other trees had but a few bricks at their roots but the mortar was there to keep the building project going.

"These trees must grow to be very strong," I thought to myself, "being so well-protected by their walls. How fortunate they are."

Time passed and my feet kept wandering among the trees in this fair land. Gradually something dawned upon my mind, the "protected" trees were withering and some were actually dying, while the trees out in the open where life could touch them were strong and fruitful. This made no sense to me and it troubled my heart and mind, until I met the Keeper of the Trees.

"Why do you build walls around some trees and why do they wither and die?" I asked. There was a sadness in His eyes and voice as He said, "Why, you are mistaken. I do not build the walls, the trees do. Each brick is a disappointment or hurt or pain. They build brick walls to shield themselves from pain, never realizing that they're actually shielding themselves from Me. The warming rays of My sun and the life-giving rain are kept out by the wall. I want them to see Me. I want them to know My love. I want so much to heal them of their pain and to bind their broken limbs but in their fear they trust the walls and do not trust Me. You see, even though the bricks hurt them, they are real to the trees and it is so difficult for them to trust in Me instead. So, I keep on shining My sun, and sending My rain to wash out chinks in their walls. And as more and more light filters in they begin to experience life and love as it should be."

He turned to go so I hurried to ask, "But why do the battered trees do so much better?" I heard Him say, as He began to walk through the wooded field, that the storms cause their roots to go down deep where they tap into His living water. Even if drought comes to the land, they do not fear, because His life is flowing in them. He was almost out of sight when I cried out, "Is there any hope then, for the walled in trees?" His reply swept over me like a wave of peace, "There is always hope, because I, the Keeper of the trees, love them with an everlasting love."

He was gone and as I pondered the things He had said I couldn't quite remember, "Were they really trees that I had seen?"

I returned again to the valley of trees. Many more now stretched their branches in praise towards their Creator, all the while sinking their roots down deep to tap into His living water. The light and love of the Keeper of the trees had broken down the walls that were destroying them and they rejoiced.

My eyes drank in the scene before me and my heart was glad, until some movement to the side caught my eye. Turning toward the disturbance of the peace I saw some trees frantically trying to rebuild their walls—even as they crumbled at their feet.

Their activity reached a frenzied pitch as mortar and broken bricks were hurriedly piled on top of crumbling walls. Some of the sickliest trees had stopped in their frenzy and now, amidst sobs and cries, clutched as many broken bricks of pain as they could to their heart. They had lived with them for so long that they became their only reality. Even though these were hurts and pains of the past and were no longer present they clung to them. In their panic they could not see that with the Keeper of the Trees taking care of them that they didn't need the bricks any more.

Perhaps the saddest trees of all were the ones whose walls were completely broken down; bricks lying crushed at their roots. Yet, in spite of their visible freedom they lived as if the walls still existed. There was no fruit, their growth was stunted and their trunks bent under the burden of pain. Fear told them that their walls were still there, that they could not trust their eyes. The only thing that lightened my sadness at seeing this scene unfold before me was to see the Keeper lovingly tending to their needs. He watered them and even made sure that His light warmed them in a special, healing way. He shielded them from the winds that might destroy them. It was painful to watch Him prune away the dead branches because with each cut the trees cried all the more. But He knew the hope of life to come. He could see beyond the moment and lovingly bathed the saddest of hearts in the healing oil of hope.

Before the scene disappeared from view I had to speak with the Keeper once more. "Why can't they see their freedom? You have broken down the walls for some of these trees and yet they are seemingly blind to the victory. What prevents them from seeing?"

Now the Keeper sat down at the roots of one of these most sad trees and rested against its trunk. Patiently He taught me about trees that day. "These trees are dying for want of love but have been so damaged that they do not recognize it and cannot accept it even when it is freely given. They have been fenced in with lies for so long that it takes time for them to see and trust *the Truth. So, I must be gentle in my care for them yet strong enough to remove the dead parts. I know it causes pain for a moment, but the rewards will overshadow it in time."*

It was easy to see that the trees were close to His heart. As He walked among them, He'd caress one, prop up the broken branch of another, and prune another; all the while singing the song of Life.

Laurie has worked very hard in therapy and has faced many fears from which she has been running most her life. I wish, as her therapist, I could say that all has come together and all is well with Laurie. But, as one very wise man once said in the first chapter of Ecclesiastes, "That which is crooked cannot be straightened." Laurie is now learning to allow God to work through the damage so that He might be glorified through her life. I believe that this verse reveals to us that it is necessary that we die daily to ourselves and allow God to reign in our decisions and behaviors.

Recently, Laurie wrote the following, which reveals to us the struggle she has in her mind and body. How many others in the Christian community are recovering as Laurie is?

"It was a wall that took many years to build. She never intended to connect the blocks into an impenetrable structure but there was too much hurt, too much confusion inside. After a time, her eyes were opened to see what she had built and she began to understand why she felt so alone, so afraid. She no longer wanted or needed the wall but the thought of taking it down was frightening, terrifying, actually. But why? So much time had passed that it became her reality, in a way her safety, because she was familiar with it. Yet it was crippling. With help, some blocks are chipped away in order to install a door. But stepping through the door causes extreme panic. She doesn't know how to function without the wall. It doesn't matter how much she understands that the wall is no longer necessary. It doesn't matter that the wall encircles her like a prison. It is all she knows. She

can't be touched, yet longs to be. In her panic outside the wall she pushes away those she wants most to be close to. She doesn't know how to ask for help. She can't get beyond the panic. So she sadly goes back and closes the door behind her. Sometimes she's afraid that she'll die there. Sometimes she's afraid she won't. Sometimes she is angry that she doesn't feel allowed to. Most people on the outside can't see the wall or its power, and they wonder why she can't function in the world. After all, all things are possible with God. The more she acts the part expected of her, the stronger the wall becomes. Hope is no longer allowed to enter. Eventually, she believes the lie that even God can't get through. She can't risk opening the door to find out."

CHAPTER 5

Louise

Over twenty years ago I met an attractive young woman, Louise, at a bowling alley. I had decided to play with a bunch of friends on a daytime bowling league. I knew absolutely nothing about the game but thought it would be fun and good for me to get out.

The first day I noticed Louise standing by herself and looking quite lonely. I walked up to her and introduced myself, and thus began a lifelong friendship.

After I moved from the area, I always kept in contact with Louise. Shortly after I moved away, she began having a lot of headaches and a lot of allergies or aversions to different foods and to most medications. She couldn't even take aspirin or Tylenol for her headaches. My friend sought relief mostly through holistic medicine. It was expensive and didn't seem to solve the problem.

About three years ago, I called Louise and asked her some questions: Do you often feel disconnected from others? Do you lose a lot of things? Does your husband tell you that you often don't make any sense? Do others tell you that they have told you things of which you have no recollection? Do you sometimes feel a much younger age? Do you feel hopeless? Do you have a difficult time sleeping? When you wake up in the morning do you still feel tired even though you have slept all night? When

37

she answered in the positive to all of them, I told her I felt that she was clinically depressed and must be holding an awful lot of emotional pain inside. She told me she had an appointment with one of the best nutritionists in the country. At this, I told her that if he was unable to help her in two months, she should please give me a call.

Two months later, to the day, I received a call on my voice mail from Louise. She sounded as though she was really feeling bad. I called her and asked her to come for a visit. She came with all of her special foods, water and other necessary items.

Louise always remembered having been sexually molested by her grandfather. Even when she talked about it, it was as if she were sharing an idea for a new dress pattern—she was devoid of emotion.

I asked her to write her story—to write about her life. During her stay with me she wrote every day and presented me with many pages which told about her life as if she were talking about someone else. I noticed immediately that her writing was filled with small details of her everyday life. She certainly did not block out much from her childhood. But what she had been able to do was to block out the emotions, the fear, the pain, the humiliation and, mostly, the anger. I believed that all these emotions, turned inward, were the cause of her many illnesses.

Following are a few excerpts from her writing; I will comment on some of them:

In the beginning God created the heavens and the earth. Then God said, "Let us make man in Our image. After Our likeness." So God created man in His own image, in the image of God, He created them; male and female. And God blessed them, and God said unto them, "Be fruitful and multiply and replenish the earth and subdue it." And God saw everything that He had made and, behold, it was very good.

You knew me before the foundation of the world; You formed me in my mother's womb. You had a plan for my life to lift others and glorify You. I was to know joy, peace, happiness and love, to be born and nurtured by a loving and caring family, to be raised on a solid foundation. A new life began September 29, 1939. A little girl, Louise, came into the world and made Irene and Bob parents. Although, You never promised us a life without testing and trials, You did promise You would be there to help us through them. And through those years You held my hand and from time to time You let me know You were there even though I wasn't quite aware of Your almighty power and grace.

The first memories Louise has are at the farm her grandparents lived on. The farm was sort of in a valley. The house had a porch along the front. Inside there was an open stairway with dark spindles on each side which came down on one side of the house. It always seemed dark inside to Louise. There was no electricity as her grandparents used kerosene lamps. Louise used to watch as her grandmother and mother would gather the lamps in one place and fill them.

One morning Louise was playing in the kitchen doorway. Daddy came in the back door. He had been out all night. He didn't say much and went in to the bedroom to change his clothes for work. He came back out into the kitchen and asked Momma if she'd pack his lunch pail. She said a few choice words and told him that if wanted his lunch pail packed he could pack his own. He then made another comment and Momma had a knife in her hand that she speared a pound of butter with and brought it up over her head. Daddy ran for the back door and went out just as she let it sail. The butter and knife hit the doorway and slid to the floor. She then opened the back door and tossed out his empty lunch pail. Louise felt kind of sad. She wished Momma and Daddy wouldn't fight.

Louise's writing is filled with little details. It's as if she didn't miss a thing—she can remember where people were standing, how dark the house seemed and all the small details of a fight between her mother and father. Many people who repress memories of abuse also repress other memories, even the good ones. As you read, you will see that the one thing that Louise does not deal with is emotion. She talks about all that happened to her as if she is reading from a newspaper. As I previously mentioned, the emotion was turned inward and caused Louise many problems as an adult, only one of them being her illness. She was also unable to connect with her husband and children as she so longed to do and as they in return needed the same connection.

There was a little boy who lived next door with whom Louise played once in a while. One time they were sitting in the grass beside the house. Somehow they began to investigate each other's bodies. (Not sure who started it.) Then Momma stuck her head out of a window over them and asked what they were doing. Louise told her "nothing." Momma came out and sent the boy home and told Louise what they were doing wasn't nice. She didn't want Louise playing with him if that is how they were going to play.

When children are small and of the same age, the act of exploring one another's bodies is not all that uncommon. Louise's mother told her that it was not nice. It is clear that this would be very confusing to Louise, as she soon shares how sexual abuse was a part of her life from a very young age.

Then one day out of nothing better to do, Louise decided to go down and run across the road when she saw a car coming. Here comes one; wait for it to get a little closer "honk'—made it across! That was kind of exciting and scary. She felt strange being on that side of the road, sort of out of her element. Here comes another car "honk"—made it back. That's enough for today. Louise did the same thing another day. This time the lady next door, Ada, must have heard and seen what Louise was up to, because she told Momma. Momma was unhappy with Louise and scolded her. She told her she could really get hurt and maybe even killed if a car should hit her. (Not sure if Louise was spanked or not).

Part of Louise is a risk-taker, needing help so desperately, it will do anything to get attention. If that was her motive, it only got her into trouble. Another reason children do dangerous things when quite small is that they feel afraid inside and need to make themselves be brave. In almost all cases we find that inside, the playground bully is a very frightened child.

Uncle Doran and Aunt Millie came to visit one evening. Everyone was sitting in the kitchen. The air raid sirens started ringing. Mom got up and pulled down all the shades and turned out all the lights. Everyone got up and went into the living room to sit because there was a small amount of light coming from the stove. Louise sat on the couch leaning against Uncle Doran. She was feeling just so peaceful and content sitting there listening to the big folks talking. When she put her ear just right against Uncle Doran's chest, his voice sounded funny. When it was time for them to go home, she wished they could have stayed longer.

I found this excerpt very revealing as to Louise's longing to be held and comforted.

The home atmosphere is a little better or Louise must be getting used to the arguments and such.
Dad has a new job with another oil-lease company on the West Notch Road. There is a medium gray shingled house that comes with the job. Louise's father drove them over so they could see where they were going to live. The house was built into a hill and had only one floor. There were three bedrooms, living room, dining room, bath and kitchen. On the front was a porch. The basement was very dark and damp. The only way to get into it was through the garage door on the outside.

The Safe Room

There are more memories at this house as Louise is getting older and remembers more.

There was a tree along the side of the house that was just perfect for climbing. Louise used to climb up and sit in the crotch of the tree. She could just sit there for hours and watch the cars go by and watch the leaves moving about. She loved being up high and feeling wind in her hair.

Today Louise finds great comfort in nature and in solitude. If she goes too long without solitude, she has a difficult time doing what needs to be done.

Mom and Dad still seemed to fight and argue a lot. Dad would either come home smashed or not come home until real late. There were nights that he would chase Louise's mother around the house. He would throw things at her and grab and push her. One time he threw a heavy metal doll bed at her that he had made the girls for Christmas. Louise and her brother and sister would hide behind the couch and chairs. It was scary.

Louise's sister and brother, Patty and Adam, were not successful in repressing their emotions and often became angry in their personal lives. Louise, on the other hand, does not allow herself to experience her emotions so in her home today, there is little fighting.

It was a Friday or Saturday night and Louise's parents decided to take Grandpa and pick up Grandma at work. She worked the night shift for Atlas Electric. They arrived a little early so they sat in the parking lot just outside the side entrance. Mom, Dad and Grandpa visited while they waited. Louise sort of listened and watched the few people that came out or went into the building. Then this whistle blew and everyone came out of the door. Grandma was surprised to see us all there. She got into the front seat with Louise's parents so Grandpa, Louise, Patty and Adam were on the back seat. Patty and Adam were

by now both asleep. Louise sat in the middle next to Grandpa.
Dad was driving out of town toward home. Louise stood up
for a few seconds then sat down, right on Grandpa's hand. It
startled her, and she said "oops" and jumped back up. Louise's
mother asked her what was wrong. Louise said, "I just sat down
on Grandpa's hand." When she sat down again the hand was
gone. (Would have thought this would have made her question
the situation later, but it didn't.) During the drive home she
happened to stand again and sure enough there was that hand
under her again. This time she didn't know what to do. She sat
there for quite a few minutes. His fingers were moving. She
finally stood up again. Next time when she sat down, she made
sure she was sitting on just the seat, and she sat there all the way
home. This was something new and strange, and she wasn't sure
what was happening.

It was time for Louise to start school. Up the road, just a wee
bit, lived a teacher. She taught in the Belleview school district. It
was worked out that Louise would ride to school with her and
her children. Louise hated school. Dad would take Louise up in
the car to catch her ride in the mornings. Sometimes she went to
school and sometimes she would cry and refuse to get out of the
car. Louise came home many mornings and got spanked. They
decided to try another friend who lived in a tiny community
called Nile. Louise was taken to her house. Same thing. Mom
and Dad were beside themselves. How were they going to get
Louise to go to school? Next year they decided to try the school
going the other way, to Dover. This time Louise was to ride the
bus that stopped for her right outside the house. Many a morning,
Mom put her on, kicking and screaming.

There was one day when Louise was attending Belleview
school she remembers quite well. It was recess time, and the class
was outside. The teacher blew her whistle for everyone to go
back inside. Louise decided she didn't want to. She ran and hid
behind the tennis courts. When she came out of hiding everyone
was inside. She went and played on the swings. Along came a
teacher and asked her why she wasn't inside. Louise told her she

didn't want to go inside. The teacher took her by the hand and took her in to her teacher. The teacher was upset with Louise and made her sit in the coat closet on a mat for the remainder of the afternoon.

Louise was not happy with school. The kids made fun of her; they picked on her one time because she wore a sleeveless dress in the winter. After that, Louise wore a sweater every day. Another time they picked on her because she wore blue and green. When it was time for recess, she never knew if they were going to let her play with them or chase her away.

Louise is crying out for help. When children suffer from abuse they often get very upset when they are put under any kind of pressure, such as school. They also try desperately to let someone know that something is wrong. All too often we ascribe bad behavior to the child and never find the root cause.

Louise started having problems being sore when she would go potty. Mom finally took her to the doctor. He gave her some medicine to apply and told Mom to sit her in some warm water every night. That didn't feel good either. Finally, after a while the soreness went away.

Thankfully, today, doctors would be more suspicious of the cause of this condition.

Grandma and Grandpa moved to another farm. Louise went to the barn with Grandpa one night while he did the chores. Grandpa lifted Louise onto a window compartment of some sort and removed her underpants. Grandpa molested Louise, and she did not know what was happening. When Grandpa finished, Louise was sore and glad it was over. They went back to the house. Louise didn't tell anyone.

There were nights when Louise had bad dreams of bombs going off and fire burning up buildings. They would wake her up. Sometimes it was hard to get back to sleep.

Louise is allowing herself to experience some of her fears and anxieties in her dreams.

One summer the next-door neighbor, who was a teacher, called Mom and asked her if Louise could come to Vacation Bible School with them. She was going to be one of the teachers. Mom agreed. There were games, Bible stories, snacks and coloring. Louise enjoyed the week.

Louise remembers the special feeling of Christmas. Dad would come home with a big tree. Mom liked the trees with the really long needles. Mom's favorite was the bubble lights. They were fun to just stand and watch. At first they were made just in clear. Later, Dad got Mom some in colors. Christmas morning there was always a doll for Patty and Louise and a truck for Adam, plus clothes. Then it would be off to Grandma's for a big gathering of all the family and more presents.

It is interesting how good memories, among negative ones, can play an important part in someone's life. Louise's home at Christmas is filled with wonderful memories of beautiful decorations and lovely packages under the tree.

There were nights Dad would still come home and he had been drinking. Mom would be upset, and they would argue. One night Dad had just sat down to the supper table. They were arguing. Dad stood up and flipped the table upside down. Another time Dad threw a dish and broke it. Mom proceeded to open the cupboards and told him she could break dishes, too. They tossed most of the dishes out of the door onto a screened in porch. Louise remembered standing in the kitchen and watching.

Louise just stood and watched. She took on the observer role when usually a little child would be crying and screaming for the parents to stop.

One day something happened between Patty and Dad's boss. He did, or tried to, molest her. Somehow Mom found out about it and told Dad. They confronted him and told him he wasn't welcome there anymore. (Think some of this was Mom's fault. Patty and Louise were allowed to wear shorts or skirts without tops. I found pictures of myself wearing a skirt with straps but no top. (I was too old for that!)

In the beginning, Dad milked the cows by hand but later invested in a milking machine. A barn cat had had some kittens. Louise had a favorite. It was white with gray tiger markings here and there. Dad had just started to milk a cow when the kitten came along and decided to sharpen his claws on the cow's hind leg. Needless to say, the cow kicked. Out went the milk pail and Dad. Dad was furious. He tried to catch the kitten but it ran away. He picked up the pail and finished milking the cow and went to dump it into the milk can. When he finished, the kitten came over. He reached down, picked it up and raised his hand. Then he proceeded to break its neck; right in front of Louise. Louise couldn't believe her eyes. She was shocked. She turned around and went out of the door. She stood outside and cried for a few minutes and then went to the house. She told her mother what had happened. Her mother didn't say much. Nothing was mentioned again about the kitten. (There was always a fear of Dad—a fear of what he was capable of when he got mad.)

When Louise came to me for counseling, her father had been living with her for almost six years. His older years had not mellowed him. It was very difficult for Louise to have him in the house and to meet all of his needs. She was again repressing her emotions which eventually made her unable to function. I told her husband that her dad had to go into some kind of assisted-living program if Louise were to heal.

Mom decided we needed more income. She got a job at Atlas Electric where Grandma worked. She worked the night shift. It was time for Louise to help with meals. Mom got things started and showed Louise how to finish things up. On occasion, when Mom worked a Saturday, Louise decided to surprise her mother and mop the floors, dust and do some ironing. Her mother was pleased and thanked her.

Today, Louise continues to feel her best when she is cooking and cleaning and taking care of the house. Even though she could well afford someone to clean for her, she has never hired anyone.

Sometimes Louise was in the barn when Grandpa did the milking. Louise's father helped Grandpa. When the milking was done, the cows were given hay, and straw was spread under them to lie on. Grandpa usually went upstairs in the barn and tossed down hay through the hay shoot. Sometimes Louise went along. It was always fun to jump around in the haymow. When they were by themselves Grandpa found a secluded place and took Louise's underpants down and molested her.

Grandpa did this on lots of occasions. One time they were in the barn and someone called for him. He closed the door and locked it, and told Louise to be quiet. When they eventually left, he molested her. Louise did not understand what it was but knew that sometimes she had a good feeling when he did these things to her. When Grandpa finished, he opened the door and looked out to see if there was anyone around; then they left.

Grandpa had an old blue truck. When it was haying season they sometimes drove it to the field they were haying in. This one day Louise was with Grandpa in the truck. They had gone ahead and were waiting for the hay wagon to come. Grandpa had Louise lie on the back seat and remove her underwear. He proceeded to molest her all the while Louise was looking at things on the dashboard. There were silver knobs and some Doublemint gum sticking out of the ashtray. In the distance you could hear the wagon coming. Grandpa helped Louise right herself and got out of the truck. They stood by the truck

Louise had learned to keep her emotions at bay and accept the abuse as something that was going to happen. It is interesting that she was aware of how good it often felt. In the above excerpt she shares how a child can focus on something else, in this case the silver knobs and the Doublemint Gum, so as not to be there. Children often do this in school when things are not good at home or elsewhere in their lives. Often they are referred to as "daydreamers" or diagnosed with ADD. In reality, they are trying desperately to keep their minds away from the very difficult conditions of their lives.

Louise got a small pair of knitting needles and some yarn for Christmas one year. Grandma taught Louise how to knit the stocking knit stitch. Louise started a small scarf but never got to finish it.

Louise still takes up the knitting needles or the crochet hook; she is excellent in these areas. She also does alterations for stores that sell very expensive clothes. Sewing to perfection is soothing for Louise as it was something she began at a very early age; it was another place to put her mind.

Grandma got really sick. A hospital bed was brought in and set up in the living room for her. She spent most of the day in bed. She loved listening to her birds and they were happy to have her there. Louise used to like to sit by her and feel the soft skin that hung down under her chin.

Louise noticed her mother just standing by the bathroom window looking out. Louise felt there was something wrong. She thought her mother might have been crying. Mom was singing a lot. Two songs Louise remembers are, "The Old Rugged Cross" and "It Is No Secret." Every weekend there was a trip to see Grandma.

Louise is a Christian today. She loves God and works very hard in any avenue that allows her to help others. One of her main activities is running a soup kitchen. From the neighbor taking her to Daily Vacation Bible School, which she enjoyed, to her mother finding comfort by singing old hymns, we see the early Christian influence.

Louise stayed home from school. Not exactly sure why. Mom was busy cleaning the bathroom. Louise was trying to find something to do in the kitchen. Mom asked her if she'd like to bake a cake. Louise got out the bowl and found a spoon. Mom began calling out the ingredients and the amounts. Louise began putting the cake together. Then Mom asked her if Grandpa had been touching her where he wasn't supposed to touch. Louise was surprised and wondered what she should say. Finally, she decided to tell her the truth. She said, "Yes." It was a relief to have it out in the open. Mom's reply was, "He did the same thing to me when I was your age. Just stay away from him. Don't be anywhere alone with him. Make sure there are people around." This surprised Louise and in some way was disappointing. She had expected her Mother to be really upset and angry and to confront Grandpa.

After that day Louise tried avoiding her grandfather as much as possible. There were still a few times he managed to catch her alone. But soon the molestation stopped.

It is obvious as we read these excerpts from Louise's writings that she has retained much of her early life. She talks about the every-day things in the same way as she shares about her grandfather's abuse; as though she is a reporter and just giving the facts.

Repression of emotions is one way of coping. The main problem with this is that you are rarely able to connect with anyone emotionally; not your spouse nor your children, as emotions are not a part of your life. Eventually, Louise's body began to suffer from all that she was holding on the inside. Her marriage and family also suffered.

But, if you were to meet Louise you could not help but like her. She is kind, very talented and runs her home almost to perfection. Her method of caring is by doing things for others, so she is quick to volunteer for things that need to be done. And whatever Louise does, she does to perfection.

As we worked together, Louise gradually became in touch with the feelings of the child and could release them in our sessions. Her headaches stopped and she was able to eat most foods. She forced herself to talk with her husband, and with a little coaching we were able to get her husband to help Louise share her feelings. He had to accept Louise's right to be angry, as I was encouraging her to allow herself to have anger and to express it. At first, expressing her anger in a calm manner was very difficult and it took some adjusting on the part of her family, who were used to an even-tempered Louise.

If you were to ask Louise the thing for which she is most grateful, she would tell you that it is that she is able to feel a part of life, to experience emotions.

CHAPTER 6

Sarah

As a child, I always pretended that I ran an orphanage. I loved all the kids and made sure they were happy. The invention of dire circumstances was a necessary part of my pretend game, because only then could I be the strong rescuer.

Of course, the game was the only way I could keep going. The truth was that I was afraid and wanted so very much for someone to love me and tell me that I was special and an important part of their lives. The only way that could happen was through my pretend time. As I write this, I wonder if my mother had to pretend, also, as a way through a very difficult childhood. Probably.

Another way I pretended was to imagine that something happened to my parents and other people adopted me. And I was a perfect child. My talents were without end. I had a beautiful voice, could play the piano better than the lady at church or Liberace himself; I was the smartest and the nicest kid in school. Everyone liked me and wanted me as their friend, and I was a wonderful friend. This game was so much fun and how I fell asleep every night after I said my prayers.

An interesting facet of this pretend game was that I always made the people who adopted me very strict, and I always had to do something that was not the best so they would have to discipline me. I didn't understand this as a young person, but

I do now. A child longs for loving discipline, because that is how the Heavenly Father created us. Just think—someone loved me enough to want me to do the right thing. They would discipline me in love. This lesson has become invaluable to me as I do parenting seminars. When this need is not met, we can see how people might allow themselves to be abused as adults. Maybe, they might think, he just loves me so much he really wants me to do the right thing.

Sarah is such a special young woman. She didn't pretend that she ran an orphanage. Actually, she had to run from danger and harm, while living in one. For a while some people took her into their home and out of the orphanage. But, it was only for a while, and when it became inconvenient, she went back.

I will let Sarah tell us her story before I comment on the ways she coped during and since this very difficult childhood:

Jeremiah 1:5 – "Before I formed you in the womb I knew you, and before you were born I consecrated you; I appointed you."

My mother grew up in a home with parents who were very strict. They frequently drank in secret and never discussed any problems. It was a very dysfunctional home.

Like many, my mother suffered personal tragedies. Besides a negative home life, she lost her fiancé to a tragic drowning accident. This and other difficulties haunted my mother throughout her life resulting in mental illness and the inability to make good life decisions.

Later on my mother met another man whom she married seven months later. They lived in the Catskill Mountains in upstate New York. My mother gave birth to three children, two girls and a boy. I was the middle child. Shortly after my sister was born, our mother took us children from the home and went to New York City to live close to her family.

There is so much I cannot remember. But, I do remember living in an apartment with my mother and siblings. One incident I recall is my mother throwing things out of the

Sarah

windows. Police officers came to the door and told my mother that it would be best if they took us. Mom screamed and tried to prevent them from taking us away from her. We were taken to a precinct.

My mother's illness resulted in her inability to raise her children, so my brother, sister and I were separated and sent to live with different family members. We were then placed into an orphanage in Manhattan.

I vaguely recall being in a crib. When I was old enough to sleep in a bed, there were beds lined up in large dormitory rooms where we slept two per bed, head to foot. The child who got into bed first was allowed to put their head at the top of the bed where there was a pillow and get the glass of water on the night table. There were "night ladies" who sat in rocking chairs and watched over us during the night. In the play area I recall a wooden guillotine used to threaten us so we wouldn't talk.

Later, I recall living once again with my mother in Staten Island in our own apartment. My mother, sister and I slept in the bed together, and my brother slept on the couch. One day my aunt and uncle came and took the three of us to another orphanage. I was introduced as the "new girl." My siblings and I were separated into different groups. My mother was admitted into a hospital and our apartment was vandalized, robbed and boarded up.

Shortly after arriving at the "home," a bowl was placed on my head and my long hair was cut off around the bowl. I was forced to eat cereal until I vomited. At night, if there was talking, we were punished by having to stand in the dark shower room with the roaches.

On "visiting Sundays," parents of some of the children came to visit. As I got older, my mother would visit but I was so angry at her that I would not meet with her. Later when I was able to visit with her, we would take buses to go on outings. Sometimes we would go to pizzerias, Chinese restaurants, diners or a park, zoo, etc.

When I was approximately six years old, the night ladies would wake the girls up at 6 A.M. for church if they wanted to go. We indicated we wanted to be woken up by tying a sock around the foot of the metal bed frame. My friend Theresa and I went practically every morning. We memorized the mass and would say it quietly with the priest. We all loved the priest, Father Kenny. He was a kind and a gentle man. He would sit about six of us (maybe more) on his lap. We'd pile up on each side and he'd tell us stories.

Whenever we drove past houses on one of our outings, I would imagine they each held a "Brady Bunch" family. I would wish I could be a fly on the wall and see what it was like to live in a house as a family.

One day a family came to the home to become volunteers. Volunteers are those who are willing to take children in their homes to visit. My brother and I were chosen and got to visit them on the weekends. I hated Sundays because then they would drive us back to the orphanage. Monday mornings when I woke up I thought I was in their home until I saw the dormitory's "EXIT" sign and the rows of beds. This made me hurt inside.

Eventually, they became my "foster parents" (at age seven); that meant I got to live with them for good. I would still be driven back to the home for "Visiting Sundays." But one very sad day we got the news that we would be returning to the home to live. After tasting family life for a few years, we were returned to the orphanage.

The home had gotten worse. Kids were brought in from prisons like Riker's Island. There were girls who used brass knuckles to beat up men counselors. It became very difficult.

Many scary memories still haunt me. I remember a boy standing on me as I lay on the bottom of a pool. I remember the high school boys chasing me, pulling my hair down to the ground and saying "I'll get you when you're fourteen. I'll get you when you're fifteen, sixteen, seventeen," and so on. Counselors beat us and told us no one wanted us, that is why we were there. (I praise God that He wanted us.)

I remember playing hooky from school, going down to the ferry terminal and giving people money to buy us liquor and getting so drunk. I once wet my pants sitting outside my junior high school in the cold. We were smoking pot and drinking. I had fights with people. I was very angry. I took subways into Williamsburg, Brooklyn at 2 A.M. Once I was chased through the Canal Street Subway Station.

A bunch of us running away from the orphanage and sleeping on broken chairs or the floor in someone's home is part of my memories. I would be hungry, fall asleep and dream of a party I heard about where we could go and get chicken and hide some in our clothes. Eventually we would be found and returned to the orphanage.

Once, when I was lying in my bed with cracked ribs from a fight, the six-foot administrator, who made it his responsibility to get the children to go to school, flipped the bed over with me in it. He did not even bother to ask why I was in the bed. This happened after having everything I owned robbed and my room destroyed.

Girls from higher groups came down and made us fight each other. They would get us out of bed and tell us whom in our group we had to fight, and if we did not, they would hit us.

When my mother would come to visit on Sundays, I would at times have black eyes and scabs on my face; these were from the counselors. I was so angry. I hated my mother for leaving me there and not protecting me. I did not want to see my mother when she came to visit on Sundays. I cursed her and avoided her.

There were many nights we went to bed hungry. A counselor, who was good to us, would go to the kitchen and ask for food. Sometimes she came down with eggs and sometimes cookies. I remember "ladyfingers."

One night when I was twelve or thirteen, about fourteen girls came to my room, woke me up and tried to trick me into coming out of my room by saying I had a phone call. Of course, my intuition warned me this was not good. I said, "Tell them I'll call them back." Well, they did not like my response and said, "If you don't get out of the bed, we'll drag you out." Why did I get stuck with a deep-sleeping roommate? I quickly calculated and decided if I got out there would be less immediate physical violence. Hindsight is 20/20. They marched me down the hall, past the counselors, and into the large bathroom. After the last person entered the bathroom, a wooden stick made in the wood shop class was placed between the door and wall so no one could get in. Jealous interrogation began then fists and feet began to meet my face and body. My head hit the wall as they punched me. I kept thinking, "Fight back! Don't be a chicken! Don't let them beat you"! There were so many, and it would only make them hit me more. Now my face and body were numb. Someone said, "Let's burn her hair." Thank God there was one who softly said, "No." I was warned not to tell anyone and, finally, let out. As the door opened, someone took the wooden pole and hit me over the head. I began to go down and did not allow myself. I began to walk, and they continued to kick me from behind.

When I got back to my room, I woke my roommate, and she held me in her arms and felt the bump on my head. She became angry. Voices came from over the cubicle and my roommate began to argue. The arguing stopped. Minutes later, buckets of ice water were thrown over the top into our beds.

Morning came and my roommate left for school, I was alone in my room. A few girls entered (all we had for a door was a curtain in the doorway). I was startled. Two girls removed scissors from their back pockets as the others held me. They cut large chunks of hair from each side of my head. They left and I cried.

One night as I sat on the window ledge of that same bathroom, at 3 A.M., I was feeling lonely, abandoned and afraid. I cried out to Jesus. I begged Him to come and sit next to me. "Please Lord, please sit next to me. I know you hear me. Please hold me, please." I don't know how long I pleaded. I truly wanted Jesus to physically sit next to me and wrap His arms around me and hold me. Psalm 10:17 says, "O Lord, thou wilt hear the desire of the meek; thou wilt strengthen their heart; thou wilt incline their ear to do justice to the fatherless and the oppressed so that man of the earth can strike terror no more."

I was sent to a group home. This is where they set up houses with fewer girls or boys to create more of a home or family-like environment.

I was in high school now, getting high on marijuana and acid.

In 1976, (I was sixteen) my brother met a group called the "Forever Family." The members of the group wore big red buttons with white lettering that read "GET SMART, GET SAVED," and my brother did. He was excited and wanted to "turn me on" to this Jesus or the group. Well, I too, "got saved." My brother remained with the group for one and a half years. They wanted me to move in with them and share dormitory-like facilities. I wanted to go to college, and I was believed not to be "committed" to the group.

At this time, my mother finally got her own apartment, and my brother and I went to live with her. I got a handshake and $500, like everyone else who left. My mother wanted to be my mommy and take care of me. I hated it. I could not be "taken care of" after having no mother and having to protect myself during my childhood. My mother continued having nervous breakdowns but now I was responsible for her too.

She would begin drinking, burning things in the oven and removing everything from the dressers in the house and the kitchen closets then building things with them. She would have all the music boxes in the apartment going at the same time. When I called the hospital, they would ask me if she were doing harm to herself or anyone else. If I said, "No," they would say that they were not responsible. I was frustrated. I had knots and a burning sensation in my stomach. I tried to get my mother to pick up her stuff and put it away. I was extremely angry, afraid and felt helpless.

One Christmas, I remember I woke up to see my mother naked under the Christmas tree. At times, I could admit my mother to the hospital. She was angry with me. My mother was on lithium and receiving electric shock treatments. I would visit her in the hospital. She was bruised all over and was very loud. When she wasn't too angry, she would drag me around loudly introducing me to the other patients.

At this time, I moved and went to live with the people who had been my foster parents.

Doing this was the epitome of BETRAYING my mother. I registered for college and received grants. I realized when I started college that I could do anything I wanted. Sitting in a three-hour lecture about cells and being stoned out of my mind was not unusual for me. I would take eighteen pages of notes but when I met someone who had missed the class and asked me what it was about, I had no idea. I decided I would try not to get high. I was taking seven sciences at once.

My foster parents' daughter had gone off to live with an older man. I ended up doing all the cleaning of their home besides working a part-time job. The cleaning and laundry never seemed to be done quite good enough. I felt like Cinderella. I decided to get my own apartment in Brooklyn as I had met a guy I really liked who lived there.

As an adult, whenever I passed houses, I wished I could feel as peaceful as I thought the houses looked. I had to keep the outside of me as noisy as the inside. I was always running. (Now, knowing the Lord, I find He gives me His peace just as He promised.)

I realized I needed some therapy and decided I'd rather spend my money fixing the inside of me than trying to look good on the outside. I was afraid of relationships and marriage; I needed to work and sort things from my childhood out.

My therapist said it was amazing that I was as together as I was with the amount of deprivation I had suffered. I knew it was the Lord who had kept me. I told this to people. Friends would ask, and I always remembered the morning I sat on that window ledge talking to Jesus.

When I traveled to New York City on the express bus to work, I sometimes heard girls speak of their fathers. I would feel emptiness. I would look at women wherever I was and think, "She looks so loving and caring, I wish she were my mother." I would explain to others, "almost everything that you want you can get," but if you don't have a mother and father, you'll never have it. Now I know Psalm 27:10, "For my mother and father have forsaken me but the Lord will take me up."

In about 1987, I placed my mother in an adult home. My mother couldn't be angrier. This blew my mind. Have we come 360 degrees? My mother put me in a home, and I was angry with her.

My mother died on January 5, 1988 of a heart attack.

At this time I was living in the fast lane; out to dinner every night, wealthy boy-friends with Corvettes, Mercedes, BMWs; staying in the plushest hotels in Manhattan; 30-foot race boats, jet skiing, snowmobiling; Broadway plays and the best and most expensive restaurants in Manhattan. Everything. I wanted to do and go everywhere; wanting to make up for what I didn't have growing up.

I got involved in a very unhealthy relationship and felt out of control. I, again, turned to God and begged Him to get me out of this relationship. I cried and begged for His help, and I also asked Him to give me a man with whom I could have a good relationship, marriage and family. Isaiah 30:19-21 says, "Yes, O people in Zion, who dwell at Jerusalem, you shall weep no more. He shall surely be gracious to you at the sound of your cry; when He hears it, He will answer you and though the Lord give you the bread of adversity and the water of affliction, yet your Teacher will not hide himself anymore, but your eyes shall see your Teacher and your ears shall hear a word behind you saying, 'This is the way, walk in it,' when you turn to the right or to the left."

Well, His promise was fulfilled again.

I met Scott. We went to church together, and I began seeking and listening to the Lord. The Lord showed how to know Him better. Scott and I married. During my first pregnancy while watching the 700 Club, I begged the Lord for forgiveness of my sins and asked Him to take me back and be my Savior and the Lord of my life.

The Word of God says in Joel 2:25, "I will restore to you the years which the swarming locust has eaten, the hopper, the destroyer and the cutter … "

The Lord has truly given me the desires of my heart. I am married to a loving, dedicated man. We have two beautiful sons, a house that is a home; good jobs have been provided and good health. I continue to have a growing and loving relationship with my brother and sister. And, so very wonderful, I have families: our family, my siblings, Scott's wonderful family and my spiritual family. And I have the peace and joy that comes from the Lord.

I'm here to tell you that there is nothing in this world that is more satisfying and fulfilling than living your life in Jesus Christ. I have had both sides. Jesus gives purpose. Even as a mother and wife, I know I am better in these areas because of Him.

I have thought about why it is so much better having God to help you in your different roles in life. Without the Lord, the world has us living lies; everything is "rush-rush," and "you're first." Make sure you are not used or taken for granted. Satan's goal is selfishness and pride. In Jesus, the goal is the opposite; acquiring the fruit of the spirit: peace, patience, and love—all of which make us better wives, mothers, relatives, friends and children of the King and heirs of His grace. As if that weren't enough, He promises us if we endure to the end, we will have eternal life with Him.

Now I understand it is only by suffering that we learn compassion, and I am thankful to the Lord for the experiences I have had. They have made me who I am and whom the Lord will use. I am excited to see how the Lord will use me to help others.

Results of an early abusive childhoold

Sarah, like many of my clients who have had difficult childhoods, came to see me because of very unstable emotions. Even though Sarah is very thankful for the many good things in her life, she continues to deal with many negative emotions that make her day-to-day living quite difficult at times.

It is important to note here that Sarah's testimony was written five years ago. She talks about how she had a two-and-a-half-year honeymoon with the Lord. Actually, one way of escape is often through becoming very religious and getting very involved with things of the church. But this will not last, and the pain of the past pushes through.

Sarah has many of the same emotions I mention in the early chapters of my book. Anger, fear, defensiveness and the need to be helpful are a few of the common emotions that become part of someone who survives childhood trauma. Sarah seems to have little control over these emotions even though some of them are not acceptable to her as a Christian.

When Sarah and I do memory work together, we come in contact with some fragments of her personality that keep us from being as successful as we would like. One of these is a very stubborn part of Sarah that we refer to as the "soldier." This part wants nothing to do with trying to remember things that have happened, and she has no trouble expressing this to me as she crosses her arms over her chest in exasperation at my questioning Sarah.

Even though the "soldier" is causing problems with the memory-work process, she was very definitely an important part of Sarah's survival. She was, and is, very protective of Sarah. It was not safe for Sarah to trust anyone; she was not able to go to anyone for help and if she did, it could have been disastrous for her. Yet, a child needs and wants someone to talk to, always hoping that someone will be there for her and rescue her from danger. The only way a child can overcome this natural need and longing is to create a part of herself that is stronger and will not allow her to be weak and to hope for rescue. Thus, we have the "soldier" who has served Sarah very well over the years. But, now we must convince the "soldier" that it is okay for Sarah to remember those things that she has not allowed herself to look at all these years. It is the necessity of keeping a secret that allows all the different coping mechanisms to stay in place, causing inner turmoil for Sarah.

Let's look at some of Sarah's other coping mechanisms. There is the little girl who always wanted to know God. Remember her? She is the one who tied a sock to her iron bed every morning so that she could go to mass at 6:30 a.m. She is the one who memorized all the masses and who loved the priest who was kind. She is still very much a part of Sarah.

But, on the other hand, where was Jesus when the young girl wanted Him to come and sit by her? Why didn't He keep her from harm? Why didn't her mother get better? Why is it that no one wanted Sarah?

Sarah can talk very easily about the dedicated Christian who is part of her, but she talks just as freely about the part that wants nothing to do with God. She can feel very guilty when the anti-God part of her acts out, but we can see why it would be necessary to have this as a coping mechanism. It is easier sometimes just to give up than to continue to be disappointed. So, Sarah developed a part of herself that told her not to count on God. He wasn't doing anything to make matters better.

We hear Sarah talking about the sexual part of herself. "If you can't beat them, join them" is an old saying. Boys were always after Sarah in the orphanage and there was no way of escape. These are some of the memories that still must come out and that the "soldier" is very reluctant for Sarah to have to deal with. Sarah refers to living on the "wild side" in order to make up for the things of which she was deprived. But, sadly, because Sarah learned one thing men wanted from her, she was unable to turn away men's sexual advances. Thus, we can see the importance of Sarah's sexual part. And living on the wild side meant allowing that part to be in the forefront for a period of time.

Of course, Sarah developed the "performer." This part of Sarah has done a lot of positive things in her life. Education became important to her, as did hard work and achievement. The "performer" is very much a part of Sarah's daily life as a wife and mother. And, important to note is that the "performer" needs to be in control, and this causes interpersonal problems for Sarah in almost every area of her life.

It is easy for us to see how necessary it is for Sarah to be in control of what happens around her. If not, she could really be hurt and unable to accomplish all that was important to her. I know that Sarah refers to herself as being too controlling at times and is concerned about the effect this will have on her husband, sons and friends. The awareness of this is very helpful. The "performer" needs to know that Sarah is no longer the helpless child. God has provided her with a husband and friends who care for her and want to be there for her. How does she learn this? This will come as Sarah continues her memory work and brings to the conscious level the things she is afraid to remember. Then she will be free to know that these things are over. The child and teenager will no longer be trapped in some scary and abusive place.

It is important for me to remind people like Sarah that it is not so much that they are trying to control others as it is they just cannot stand the feeling of being out of control.

When Sarah, or anyone who has repressed emotions or memories of childhood abuse, becomes overwhelmed in any area of her life, she will come in touch with the child who was so out of control. She will experience her fear and sadness and will immediately begin using the coping mechanisms she developed as a child to get away from this fearful and sad part of herself.

Now, I come on the scene as Sarah's counselor and tell her that God wants truth in the innermost parts. I want Sarah to embrace the one that is fearful and sad. If not, she goes into the constant self-rejection mode that I talked about in the opening chapter. How can she present herself before God, asking Him to work through her and in her, when we reject parts of ourselves?

We see this in God's Word in many places, but David and Peter are very good examples. David did not present to God the hurt and emotionally abused child of his past. He was busy being used for God's glory. The "performer" was out and doing all God asked of him. But, what about that little boy whose father did not consider significant enough to present to Samuel as a son that might be God's anointed one? And, the young lad whose older brother, Eliab, made fun of and rejected. What happened to him? It is evident that when David had things pretty much under control and the kingdom was doing well, he got in touch with something. He needed to meet a longing within. Was it to feel significant? How could he not feel that way? Isn't it interesting how people strive their whole lives for significance and safety? And just when they think they have arrived, they learn that nothing is there at their destination point. It is like the very successful businessman who told me, "Carol, all my life I wanted to get to the top. Well, when I finally got up there, I found there was nothing there." What did he hope to find there? Was it a feeling that only God can give? The ability to be content where we are eludes most of us; we seem to be on a constant search for the mysterious "answer."

It is not uncommon for people to tell me that the need to understand what happened to the child is ridiculous. We are adults, the past is over, and now "we belong to Jesus." I ask them, "Does the child belong to Jesus? If you are not aware of the child, does he belong to Jesus?"

Perhaps it is my age, but I feel compassion for people who need to tell others what they should and should not allow to bother them. I am sure as you read that sentence you can see the absurdity in it. These people are judging themselves, putting themselves in "should" boxes. I hear it from the women in Bible study all the time. They say things like, "I know I shouldn't let this bother me." I suggest that a better use of their energy and thought processes would be to ask why it might bother them.

Wouldn't it be terrible if Christians who did not know Sarah's story began telling her what feelings and behaviors were appropriate for her if she were indeed a Christian? Aren't we ever so grateful that Jesus told us not to put the pressure on ourselves of deciding about another's walk with Him?

How is Sarah doing today? Well, the "soldier" is beginning to allow us access to the repressed stories of her life. Hopefully, before this book is completed, the causes of her emotional ups and downs will be revealed so that healing can begin.

Another young woman I know tells me that she realizes that she can't allow others to get really close to her because they will find out that her life is not altogether as she portrays it. This young lady has a perfectionist part to her personality that has to do the best at everything. If there is too much outside pull, she gets overwhelmed and can't achieve perfection. So, she carefully orchestrates her social life and decides just how close to allow others to get. It gets lonely, but the intimacy is not worth risking a "breakdown" in the system. Part of this is true with Sarah, but also she has strong walls around the essence of who she is, to protect her from harm. This prevents the closeness to others that she would like to experience.

Sarah also refers to fragments within herself that do not agree. One longs for intimacy and closeness; one builds walls. One likes to help others; one longs for help. One wants to serve God; one is really frustrated with the thought of a "Good God." There is constant turmoil and people like Sarah always find themselves trying to regroup. It is very tiring.

Sarah found it hard to "hear" or "remember" the information she received in counseling. This is due to so much scattering inside her mind. Often when a client feels safe with her therapist and has held down her child's need for safety, she hears things as a child, not as an adult. You have read about Sarah's various parts and how they developed into what I refer to as her "system." These parts can hear things differently or not at all. As Sarah's negative memories surface and the need to keep secrets recedes, she will have cooperation on the inside. This is happening more and more as I work with Sarah.

Other therapists, pastors or helpful friends reading this book can relate to the thankfulness I feel when I get warm and loving messages from these wonderful "Daughters of the King." We are truly more blessed when we give to others.

Recently Sarah asked why God didn't put people in her life who would love her and be concerned about her. I reminded her that she often sabotages relationships. The child cannot trust, because there never was anyone to trust. I suggested that she might look at the past years and see whether there has been a tendency to sabotage relationships.

As I close this chapter, I wonder if you might know someone who seems to be struggling. You feel they shouldn't be; they should have it all together by now. I hope that Sarah's story will cause you to pray for that person and ask the Holy Spirit to make you an instrument of healing in his or her life.

CHAPTER 7

Release Through Writing

Many children and adults use writing as an outlet for things that overwhelm them. This was the case for Sandy, a wonderful teenager whose intelligence and determination caused me to take stock of my own behavior when faced with a difficult situation. She taught me much.

Sandy wrote this poem when she was about to leave home, where she had no freedom to "be." She aligned herself with the fern that was there year after year, enduring along with her.

Fern

Frail leaves withdrawing and curling, she fades,
Cruelly denied of benevolent shade.
Water is plentiful for she, who thirsts,
But, by her environment, she is betrayed.
Touch her, she crumbles; brown stalks naked, bare,
Save few spindly leaves not yet burnt by the air.
No ear gives heed to her crackling sobs,
Her pain not perceived by the dumb eyes that
stare.

This is protection. A haven from frost.
Would she choose protection if she knew the cost-
(Not to say that was given a choice)-
Exchanging a quick death for hell's own exhaust?

They'll move her, they promise, when springtime is
come,
Outside she'll see freedom when winter is done.
But freedom from indoors is not what she seeks,
Just simple relief from the heater and sun.

Feeling her pain as I do in my bones,
Unwilling to help her—then I'd be alone,
I wait for the springtime release from our hell,
When I will bid them a most joyful farewell
And rescue that fern and strike out on my own
To someplace that's shady, away from that heat, with
just enough
Water, and there we will grow in freedom, which
now is too far and unknown.

Another young woman, Clare, with whom I worked, used poetry to explore her feelings. She brought all her writings to my office one day, wanting me to read them. She had suffered a very abusive childhood, married young, and was finding it difficult to care for her two small children. Here are a few selections of her writings.

Brown Paper Me

Against a winter grey backdrop
Like some giant stringless kite,
Glides a bird so effortlessly
Over a field of white.

How I wish to be as that bird
And see the world he sees.
I'd give anything to soar against a cloud
Instead of being one.

Or be as the golden sun
Which brings life and warmth and mirth—
Stretch my soft, gentle rays to the whole world
And touch both ocean and earth.

Why can't I be like the sun?
Whose light shimmers on all seven seas?
Why do I have to be a lonely, sad woman?
Why do I have to be me?

With soft brown hair and curious dark eyes
Fashioned from my flesh and bone,
My beautiful daughter grew under my heart,
Whose presence makes my house a home.

I almost envy the things she'll learn.
I envy her all she can be.
The thing that I'm most grateful for,
Thank God, she won't be me!

Egg and Sperm

The egg and sperm that should never have joined
Are the ones that created me.
I'm sorry to tell you your business, Lord,
But I'm quite unhappy you see.

I don't mean to seem ungrateful.
You've blessed me with a lot.
But the one thing that I want the most
Is the thing I never got;

To hear my father say, "I love you"
And be safe within his arms.
Just to know he'd never hurt me,
That he'd keep me from all harm.

Instead he cursed and beat me
When I stepped out of line.
He never said he loved me
And was always less than kind.

I would've loved him, Jesus.
He would have been so proud,
But he's dead and I'm all broken.
Why were these things allowed?

Loneliness

Everybody needs a friend,
This is no great shame,
Even I have one best friend,
Loneliness is her name.

She goes wherever I go,
Even in a crowd.
We watch as people laugh,
That's when she's most loud.

We've always been together.
I know that this sounds strange.
But we've been friends since childhood.
Some things never change.

I do look for others;
Real friends to make and then
They either move or hurt me
And Loneliness is back again.

With Loneliness as my best friend,
I never have to fear
The chance someone will hurt me.
In fact, no one comes near.

Little Girl

A sad and lonely little girl
Lives within my soul.
A victim of the beatings,
The lies that she's been told.

She's just so sweet and gentle.
A loving little sort,
Who longs just to kindle
The love in someone's heart.

How often I have seen her
Wander to and fro
Crying, "Someone love me.
Please do not let me go."

Oh, Claire, I do love you
And I have felt your pain,
Have seen the tears flow from your eyes
As heavy as the rain.

So come to me my child.
I'll hold you close to me.
Rest your head against my heart,
I'll protect you, don't you fear.

You, after all, are me.

Together

I know that you don't know me
Though I know you all too well.
I saw all the hurt inflicted on you
And there was no one you could tell.

I saw all the tears you shed,
The loneliness you felt.
I'm aware of all the things you've done
When there was no one you could tell.

And, child, there are parts of you
That make up who we are.
We have all looked out for you,
Which is how you got this far.

It's time you got to know us,
But please don't be afraid.
See, the door is opened and the lights are on.
The foundation has been laid.

I will help you and protect you.
Together we'll help you see
All the beauty and good within you.
And together we'll all be free.
I love you, child.

This young woman's writing shows that she was well aware of her dissociation. Together we worked with her various "alters." We learned to appreciate their unique skills. The alters also got to know each other; this helped her a great deal. For example, we often counted on the stronger parts to help the child who was in so much pain.

This client was previously diagnosed by her psychiatrist with DID—Dissociative Identity Disorder. She told me that she was not able to do memory work and face the pain of the past. Thus, memory work was a very small amount of our work together.

CHAPTER 8

Ann

As I watched Ann come into the room, I could envision the other girls in the group looking to her as a leader. There is something about the way she presents herself that draws others to it. If I had to say what I thought it was, I believe it is the candor that is so much of a part of her.

Ann's early childhood years were spent in a volatile home with a lot of conflict and very little resolution. She was one of five children, all of whom have reacted in a negative way to the lack of safety in their early years.

Ann was a fighter. She would often throw herself into the conflict between her parents only to wonder later if that was the wise thing to do. She eventually went outside the home as an escape. Substance abuse and negative behaviors such as promiscuity and rebellion against parental control were ways of escaping the painful and unsteady feelings inside, but Ann later chose coping mechanisms that would serve her better in life. She got a degree in biology and went to work in a pharmaceutical company where she advanced to a management position.

Ann's coping mechanisms are: confrontation (anger), performance, and humor (sarcasm). Two of her siblings who were genetically more emotional than Ann escaped their pain through substance abuse and continue to struggle with addictions to this day.

In her journals, Ann writes:

The Book

"*Frustration. Several key pages that I wrote to be included in the book were erased from the computer and I can't find the floppy that I saved them on since the move. And who knows if I'll ever find it. Also frustrating, is that I gave copies of one particular entry to several people all of whom no longer have their copy. Darn. I can't just rewrite that entry because I was emotionally healing while writing it, I believe. And you just can't recapture that kind of emotion again—or can you?*"

My Story

"*Born on July 25, 1961, at 4:22 A.M. in St. James Hospital in Newark, NJ, to my parents Robert John Seaman and Alice Jane Campbell. My dad is third generation in this country from Italian ancestry. My mom's folks were from the south— Louisiana and Kentucky, with English, Welsh, German and American Indian ancestry.*

My dad's father was an alcoholic and had problems with rage and infidelity. He died when he was in his sixties of mouth and throat cancer after being sober for many years and having a seemingly good relationship with my grandmother. I was twelve years old. I cried for my grandfather on the back porch of the funeral home in the dark where no one could see me. Unfortunately, when my cousins saw me they could tell that I had been crying. I denied it. Although I saw my grandmother wail and my aunts crying, I did not feel like I could cry, too. I often was told not to cry. I don't know why. I cried a lot at night in the dark when I was alone.

It's funny to think of it now, but I always knew deep down inside that we are really all alone in this world, and only God could be connected to us in the deep, deep recesses of our heart, of our soul. But then I grew up and forgot that only God can fully and deeply satisfy us and I painfully tried to fill that incredibly tangible void with all the wrong things. But God is so faithful and he never gave up pursuing me and wooing me back into a relationship with Him. That just amazes me. God's love amazes me, and the more I learn about how He loves me, the more I want to be like Him and love others—with the first recipient of my new and glorious loving going to my husband. My poor husband. Well, that's another topic I'll approach later.

I read not too long ago that Mother Teresa said if we would spend one hour a day in praising God, we would have no troubles. Maybe she should say our troubles would not trouble us. I think she is right.

My grandmother Seaman is alive and living alone in Hightstown, NJ. She is eighty years old and probably should hand in her driving license. She doesn't get about as well as she used to due to hip and leg and back problems. But, she is still feisty and still very beautiful and still gets a tan and is very bitter about her life. Maybe it's paranoia more than bitterness come to think of it. Well, whatever it is she is the least thankful person I know. She is very worried about having enough food, is about a hundred pounds overweight, and hoards enough food in the house to feed a family of five for a full year. Her freezer and refrigerator are always packed with food, and to get at anything is like moving a piece of a puzzle."

We can see from her writing that Ann has turned to God as a way of coping with the life that has been so affected by her past.

In the early chapters of this book I pointed out how we develop certain coping mechanisms as a child and continue to use them as adults. This can cause us a lot of grief. One of Ann's coping mechanisms was the "performer," and it is obvious that this has been a positive for Ann. But, what happened to all the pain that the "performer" allowed Ann to block out? Well, it went inside her. The evidence is the anger and negativity that Ann often expresses, especially to those closest to her. Ann writes:

"I wonder if I have to let out a certain amount of negativity in my life because my life would be so unusual now without it since that was the sustenance of my childhood. This is not said to insult my parents nor to criticize them, rather I state it as a fact."

Journal Entry #1 Date: Saturday 11 Feb 95 Time: 23:04

"Why do I wait?! I'm beating myself up, and I just chewed on Jeff as a starving lion attacks his prey. It was ugly. I sinned; Jeff did not. Where are you Holy Spirit when I desperately need you? I'm crying and typing and feel like a jerk. No. That's JERK! I just verbally abused the man I love most in my life. And whom I love to hate sometimes. I exploded. I tried—barely, to maintain composure; then when my husband did not even acknowledge me, I lost it. My words were filthy and full of hatred, frustration and fear."

Ann married a young man who is also a product of a volatile home. Neither of them saw parents who were loving and affectionate to each other or their children. Is it any wonder that Ann and her husband put each other down and fight openly? It seems evident to me that they were programmed to behave in this manner.

As she writes in her journals, we hear Ann crying out for God's help:

"Lord, don't forget about me. Please don't leave me alone for a second—I'm sure I'll blow it on my own. Take control of my tongue. Make it very hard for me to say anything unkind ever to anyone. Please help me Lord. Please show me You care, You hear my tears and You are working it all out for good and Your glory. Amen."

It is obvious to me as I read the things that Ann writes, that she is at a loss when it comes to controlling her outbursts of unkind words. Ann's and Jeff's parents did not show affection for each other, buy presents for each other, laugh together, or go out for romantic evenings. They did not model a preference for each other's well being. Ann and Jeff heard their parents saying unkind and angry words.

In her fragmented fashion, Ann strives to pull from Jeff the very things she needed from her parents as a little girl: love, safety and significance. And Jeff, having the same needs, wants desperately for Ann to supply them for him. He uses passive-aggressive behaviors to try and achieve this. The things that Ann needs for him to do around the house often go unattended. Withdrawing from Ann, especially when she is caustic, is his way of coping. This only leaves Ann feeling more and more alone.

Anger and Negative Behaviour as a Young Person

As an adult, Ann continued to use coping mechanisms learned and developed as a child. But, besides using alcohol and drugs in her teen years, Ann felt a need to hurt herself in other ways.

One Wednesday night Ann brought the following journal entries to Bible study. She could not read them herself, so one of her best friends took on that difficult task. It was a painful cleansing for Ann, and one that I felt was directed by God. As her friend read the words that would expose Ann's soul to all of us, the women began to cry, and some got up to sit at Ann's feet. The love and power of God were very evident that evening. Her friend read:

Sunday 08, Feb 98 9:30 P.M.

"I attended the Women of Faith conference this weekend: "Bring Back the Joy". It was fabulous. Why? God spoke to my heart in a way that I don't often hear. I have been praying that God would let me know anything that stood in the way of our relationship. He did this weekend. I am confronted with my past and how ashamed I am of who I was and what I did. But why

don't I ever look at my past with compassion and sympathy to the possible reasons behind the terrible things I did? I'm not used to grace from God, let alone giving myself grace. God's grace. He has seen the unedited movie of my life and loves me anyway. He saw me through each experience of my wretchedness, and cared for me. He loves me now exactly where I am although I fail Him. He loves me. If only I can plant my feet so deeply into His love that I would not be swayed. If only we all recognized our true worth in Jesus Christ, then the word petty would be removed from the dictionary.

What do I hide in the archives of my shame? Abortion. I have shared with many people that I have experienced abortion. But I leave out a little detail. I have had four abortions.

I breathe a long sigh of relief. My secret is out. I have written it down in black and white. I have confessed to my husband. I offer it to God and although I have prayed for His forgiveness, and my babes' forgiveness, I find it so hard to forgive myself. You see I knew that abortion was wrong. Doing it once when you're a teenager can be rationalized. But repeating the act three more times was like spitting on God's face. But it was really my own face I spat on. I hated myself. I came to a place where I cut off my emotions, yet I wanted to some way almost torture myself; a form of punishment. I cannot tell you the tears I've shed, the tears I still shed.

One time when I had an abortion, I don't know for sure whether or not I was actually pregnant. Back then pregnancy tests were not as sensitive as they are today. And upon physical exam the doctor could not confirm pregnancy either. I made him do the abortion anyway. It was my own form of discipline. And I never took anything for the pain, I reasoned that I well deserved the pain and therefore, should feel everything. I was told that I would be an excellent candidate for natural childbirth.

Having a baby someday I believed would somehow vindicate my killing my other babes. I'm not sure how I thought not killing a baby would make up for killing one, but I did. For a long, long time I thought that God would punish me and not give me a *baby when I finally married and wanted to become a mommy. Getting pregnant with Thea was a very big deal for me.*

But in hindsight I can see that it was also a very stressful time for me as my past surfaced and the guilt and shame were all there playing some bad stuff inside my head. And I never admitted to any doctor that I had had an abortion until I was pregnant with Thea. But I would never admit that the number was four. The only reason for me even telling that I had had one abortion was for Thea's safe delivery. I figured one or four didn't make a difference, at least they would know I had an abortion, should that information be needed and useful in the event of a problem.

Holding my newborn baby in my arms intensified my shame. Yet I wrestled with knowing that I was forgiven and that to God my sins existed no more. Maybe I used the shame of my past to have a reason to hold on to my self-condemnation. Sometimes for what seems to be no apparent reason, I will just have the thought that I hate myself. Why? I am now working on changing the tapes that I play inside my head. I want to try to understand why I would still feel this after being with Christ for about eight years now.

I spoke with Carol last night, calling to say hello and all that. No, I called with the agenda of needing to tell someone what God was wanting to purge from my heart yet I didn't feel free to share it with Carol either now that I am thinking about it. I think I didn't feel comfortable talking to Carol about it because first of all I hate to ever say it. Second, I did say to Carol once before years ago and Carol instructed me to write each baby a letter. I never did and felt guilty over that too! I felt that if I wrote about it, even in my journal, that it would be true, which it is, and that it would be too painful to visit. Besides the fact that someone might read it and find out my ugly secret. Ugly. It is ugly what I did, yet I am not her now. I want to hold her and tell her that it's okay now, God hasn't left you, and He never did back then, either. And He wants to heal her. I want to hold her and let her cry on my shoulder for she only cried on the boyfriends' shoulder and they were not loving shoulders. She cried alone. Someone wrote in my high school yearbook my senior year: "Laugh, and the world laughs with you; cry, and you cry alone." I already had the crying part of that motto etched in my soul. And I did cry alone for a very long time.

Telling this secret of mine is painful and liberating. Now I can begin to look upon that girl in my past with love and compassion and heal me.

God's desire for us is to be whole. He gave us a variety of ways out of our problems when He knew it would allow us to survive. I don't mean abortion was a way out of my problem, rather I am referring to splitting off a part of myself, leaving her in New Jersey and moving to the west coast. I have hated parts of who I was, instead of learning to understand and ultimately accept who I am now in relation to my past.

Right now I feel tired, but a good tired. I'm so excited about God healing me and maybe allowing this part of my story to help heal others.

One of my favorite poets is Emily Dickinson. She has a poem that echoes so beautifully Christ-like love.

> *If I can stop one heart from breaking,*
> *I shall not live in vain;*
> *If I can ease one life the aching,*
> *Or cool one pain,*
> *Or help one fainting robin*
> *Unto his nest again,*
> *I shall not live in vain.*

This is how I feel about my life. If my experiences can be turned into something good, even if I don't see how, then my pain won't all be in vain. Like God says in Romans 8:28, "God works all things together for good for those who are called according to his purpose."

Jeff was really wonderful last night when I told him what I have been carrying inside me for such a long time. I walked with a lighter step today. I am so very thankful to my Lord and Savior Jesus Christ. How can I ever thank Him enough. I pray that God will use my life anyway that He wants. I want so much to be faithful to Him. I pray that He would give me faith—and every gift that He has for me and that He would teach me to use my gifts for Him. Dear Lord, teach me to love me and to love others the way You love me. Amen."

From reading the above we can see that indeed God is reaching and teaching many wonderful things to that young girl within Ann. But, what is so marvelous is that Ann has decided to take steps toward accepting herself, understanding how a young girl could do things that would hurt herself, and allowing God's grace and love to be extended to that part of herself. I call this process "gathering," the gathering together of yourself and presenting it to God.

From working with Ann as a client and experiencing her friendship which is so rich and full, I have noticed that she can easily become burdened for others and want very much to help them. If she is concerned enough, she can, almost without thinking, use some of her coping mechanisms with them. This may not be the best way to get the desired results. It is not unheard of for Ann to tell the husband of a friend that he is being a "jerk" and doesn't know how to love his wife or his family. I can certainly appreciate her loyalty and love for her friend, but these methods don't work very well.

How did this aggressive "caregiver" come about? When she was young, Ann was often put in charge of her siblings. This was especially true in troublesome times. Ann writes:

"As I am sitting here, writing this and remembering, I can recall standing in the living room of our house on South Washington Avenue. I remember watching and listening to my mother drive out of the driveway like a mad woman and peel out down the road while my two younger sisters standing next to each other in the picture window under the sheer curtain

are crying. Right before my mother left the house, she would yell at us and say that she wasn't coming back. It was an awful way to say good bye to us kids. And she was only going out to play bingo for the evening. I can feel some of the emotions of that memory now, especially when I try to imagine doing that to Thea and Amy. And I cry. I didn't cry then, at least not in front of my sisters. I was trying to comfort them and get them to settle down. I would wait until I went to bed at night and then cry myself to sleep. A frequent memory of my childhood is crying in bed at night alone in the dark and praying to God. I remember thinking about who God's parents were."

The need to help loved ones who were hurting was imposed on her when she was a small child. One can only imagine the pain she must experience when those around her are in emotional need. This need taps into the child's deepest fears: being trapped, helplessness, and one of the worst fears, that it is all her fault. Wanting to help others is a good thing, but releasing anger upon those she perceives as causing the pain is not the way to accomplish this goal. The child grew up seeing aggressive behavior in those around her. Ann writes:

"When my mother went out to play bingo, which she did many nights during the week, if my father was watching us as if no one was watching us; until he needed to intervene and he only did so in a fit of rage. This is exactly the place where I learned my way of letting anger out through rage."

Adding to this problem is the fact that Ann's parents made her feel responsible for her siblings' mistakes. She was told their errors were due to her poor example. It is easy to see how Ann would continue to blame herself for anything that went wrong with her family or those she loved. This would only increase the need for the defensive coping mechanism of anger.

The Dreaded "C Word"

In the midst of a turbulent marriage, Ann learns that she has cancer. How will this terrible disease affect this woman already struggling so hard to make her life count for God?

My Breast Cancer Experience

"*First, a few words about me before I share some of my experience with breast cancer. Because of my family background coupled with my personality temperament, it would be helpful for you to understand a little bit about the person that I used to present to the world. I have been known to come across as a woman who was self-assured, arrogant, matter-of-fact, low on emotion, high on thinking. I did not cry easily.*

Diagnosis: No one can ever prepare you to hear the words, "You have cancer." No one can know for sure what their response will be to a terrible event in their life. I found a lump while taking a shower. Two weeks later I went to my gynecologist. The next day I went for my first mammogram, and the day after that I met Dr. Sharon Andrews. During my mammogram, when the technician came back in to take more films I knew in my heart that I was in trouble. After briefly speaking with the radiologist, and before getting dressed, I immediately asked to use the phone and called the breast surgeon's office to request an appointment, informing them that I had an abnormal mammogram. After Dr. Andrews examined me we spoke in her office and she went over my mammogram films with me. She told me that my breast lump required a biopsy. I asked Sharon what her gut feeling was about the lump and she prefaced her response by saying that she could be wrong and has been wrong in the past, but that her gut feeling was that I had cancer. Tears immediately came to my eyes.

From June 12, 1995 Journal Entry:

"*Jeff told me that when he sees girls in the mall he gets angry. He said he feels angry that this cancer thing happened to me, and wonders why it had to be me. I think he is lusting after those sweet young and beautiful girls, and is angry that he is stuck married to Frankenstein's wife! After all, I hardly have a body now that anyone would crave. I cry over the loss of my beauty. A glorified body never sounded so sweet.*

I cry lying in bed at night. I wonder if I chose the right surgery. Forget the pain of it, it is just ugly. Now I am truly scarred everywhere on my body—from my face to my belly. The facial scars are from childhood accidents.

In my breast that was reduced, I still don't have any sensation in the nipple. I don't think it will return, although my doctor said that it should. But my oncologist says that my period should return in a few months and it still hasn't either. I cried last night thinking again about the fact that I now may be infertile. Oh, how I thank God that I have Thea, but to have my fertility lost is just that: a loss. In some ways I think that having had Thea makes that loss harder, not easier because now I know what I am missing.

I don't want all of my suffering to be in vain. I want good to come of it. I want my faith in God's goodness to grow. I want a marriage that even breast cancer cannot destroy. I want all of my relationships to improve and grow as a result of this experience. I want to be happy everyday, not sad. I want to focus on the bigger picture in life. I want to enjoy all of the little things in life that make it especially sweet. I want to be a wonderful mommy to my daughter, a great friend to my friends, a sweet wife to my husband, and a good and faithful servant to my God. Lord help me to be all that You desire for me."

Ann continued to use coping mechanisms learned as a child. She was a fighter—she was not going to give in. She used the "performer" part of her personality, and as soon as she was able, she returned to the work force. She did not need to work to meet the financial needs of her family or to assure future employment, as extended leave was available. But keeping busy was a trusted way to handle difficult situations. Today, because of her own struggles with cancer, she wants desperately to be there for others who are fighting cancer. It is not unusual to find Ann at the hospital bed of someone dying of cancer. She has been with cancer patients through a great deal of the destruction caused to their bodies. She shares her love, her compassion and her Savior with them.

Her desire to have another child became greater than her fear of the cancer returning. We read in her journal:

"Today is my twenty-ninth week of pregnancy. My baby is getting big and its movements can be felt from one end of my belly to the other! I am so happy and afraid at the same time. I think I need to invest in waterproof mascara, as tears streaming from my eyes is a common event. Happy tears, sad tears—tears of joy more often. I cried the first time that I heard my baby's heart beat at nine weeks. I cried when we found out that I conceived. I know I will cry the moment this baby is born.

We see Ann on a never-ending search to find herself. It is important to inject here that this is always a part of people who have repressed memories or emotions. They are forever on a search to find their true selves. Some of the things that Ann has written are things she kept from her conscious mind.

Who am I now?
I am hot tears on a friend's face who can feel someone's pain as their own.
I am an impatient mother who loves her children so much and is afraid that they really won't know how deep that love is. (And that I won't be around long enough to give them my legacy of love.)
I am the denier of the Holy Spirit who continues to prompt me yet I rarely listen.
I am a survivor.
I am an old friend to pain.
I am a newer friend to happiness, peace and joy.

*I am learning that joy isn't pain-free, and happiness
isn't joy, and peace can be in the presence of chaos.
I am a beautiful woman whose shell is decorated with
souvenirs from battles encountered; battles that have
passed but may not yet be won.
I am an ugly woman whose tongue lashes out
undeserved punishment too quickly and with much
guilt.
I am a seeker.
I am His child. I am so thankful to be His child."*

She begins to come in touch with her anger and expresses
it freely:

*"And now I feel angry about losing my breast. I'm mad
that my body is disfigured. It is disfigured. Plain and simple,
and ugly. No, I don't mean that I'm ugly, nor that my body is
ugly. It is ugly to lose a breast. Cancer is an ugly disease, for
the most part. I really do want to be used by God and to have
good come out of this experience. And I believe good is coming
out of this. But, it hurts. It makes me so sad. It makes me mad,
too. Time will greatly help move me through all of this—time
and God's healing hand. But sometimes that big dark sky up
there seems empty, and prayers seem unheard. Why does God
give us so many feelings but then tells us to not listen to them? I
really don't understand His ways. Going through life's struggles
can be confusing at best."*

Ann confronts fears about recurring cancer and her reaction
to anything that does not seem right inside her body.

*"November 23, 1995 marks the one-year anniversary of when
my breast cancer journey began. It's not over. It may never be
over this side of eternity, and that is a scary thought. I don't
trust my body. I get a headache and think, brain cancer. If my
back gets sore, it's bone cancer; soreness near my chest scars—*

recurrence at the mastectomy site! These thoughts are fleeting and don't get stuck in my head, yet they can rock your boat and temporarily rob your peace. God is good. I had a vision of Jesus Christ waiting to greet me at the top of a beautiful snow-covered mountain. Jesus was dressed in the latest ski fashions and was wearing top-of-the line ski equipment. He is holding skis for me and waiting to take the first run down the mountain with me! I smiled through tears imagining this scene.

I want to think about heaven (or the new earth) more. What the heck do you do with an eternity? What does it mean or look like to worship God for an eternity? I don't know how to truly worship God now for an hour, let alone an eternity. And yet He pursues us! Amazing."

I cannot help but wonder how difficult it was for the little Ann to handle the scary things that happened in her home. It is evident that she uses those techniques developed in early childhood in her battle with cancer. It is also evident to me that she continues to experience the aloneness and fear of the child.

Ann has a very compassionate heart. It hurts her that some of her siblings engage in substance abuse to avoid the unhealed pain they experienced as children. Reflecting on their addiction, she writes in her journal:

"Cancer pales next to substance abuse. Everything in life is hard without Jesus. Can't imagine living without Him now. I used to wonder why more people didn't drink or do drugs who were without the Lord. I mean what's the point to life without God?! Why bother? Life is so meaningless any other way than with Jesus Christ.

So how am I doing now? Ok. I'm getting better and better, although I would like the healing to speed up. Why is patience not something that is inherent in our character? My hair is growing back and that is wonderful. I can't wait until I need a haircut! I've been using shampoo on my fuzz even though I really don't need to; I just like the idea of shampooing my hair. Small pleasure in life."

At each of our Bible studies, I have the opportunity to see and hear these wonderful women pour out their hearts and souls to one another and to God. I watch as they become a part of one another's healing.

When her mother learned she had ovarian cancer and that the outcome was bleak, I could sense the concern and compassion Ann had for her mother and the flickering of added fear. Her mother's cancer points to a greater risk of the return of cancer in Ann's body. All the women in Bible study have committed to pray and stay close to Ann.

Tuesday 31 March 98, 10 P.M.

"My mom has cancer—ovarian. We found out today after she had surgery to remove a large mass (6" x 6") from her abdomen that was engulfing her uterus and ovary. The surgeon, Dr. Jackson, said that the operation went well and that he was able to remove everything as the cancer was confined to one area. However, due to lymph node involvement, mom's cancer is Stage III.

I believe that we have the BRCA1 gene in our family in light of breast cancer diagnosis in my Aunt Helen (at age twenty-seven), my cousin Terry (at age thirty-two), and myself (at age thirty-three), along with my mom's diagnosis of ovarian cancer. But what of it?

Dr. Jackson said that mom would need chemotherapy. My dad asked the doctor what her prognosis was and he simply said that one third of patients will do well with chemo and the other two thirds will have problems. Vaguely clear, clearly vague. Statistically, she has a 33% chance of doing well with chemo, and a 67% chance of not. Drop statistics. Only our dear Lord knows the big picture including our departure date. But I'm scared. I don't want to see my mom suffer. Yet I have seen her suffer her whole life in one way or another. Maybe as Carol said, she will be open to receive love and healing in her life and quiet all the angry children running around inside of her that control her life.

(cont'd. Wednesday 1 April 98, 9:30 A.M.—wish I could say "April Fool's mom.")

When my dad and I, along with my Aunt Jeanie (and her friend Tony) went up to my mom's room when she was released from recovery, I asked my dad how he wanted to handle breaking the news of her cancer to her. He didn't know and asked me what to do. At first I felt lost as to what to do, but then immediately knew: if she didn't ask, don't tell her just yet as she was still coming out of anesthesia; and if she did ask, tell her the truth.

She asked immediately. I looked at my dad waiting for his response to my mom's simple question of "what was it?" only to see his paralyzed expression. I answered: it's cancer, I'm sorry. My mom seemed to stop breathing while the harsh reality of her greatest fear settled upon her. Then she said to me, "why are you sorry?" I'm sorry that I have to tell you this, was my reply. I cried. We exchanged I love you's and I left.

Since I am a cancer survivor, it seemed right that I should be the one to give the bad news because it doesn't have to be all bad news in the long run. This I know to be true and not just because I did not die.

Lord, please help my mom and dad and family feel and know the power of Your love in times of trials. Help her, Lord, to know how much You care for her and are ever present.

Thank You, Lord. Amen."

God has a way of meeting a need in us, often through very difficult circumstances. I have seen Ann's mother free to be weak and to need her children's love and the love of others in her family. She has an excuse not to have to be able to do everything and to control everything. What a relief that must be. Ann and her mother have drawn closer together, and Ann's mother has grown closer to God.

Ann shared with me a recent letter she got from her mother. I find it both beautiful and sad.

Ann's mother writes:

Dear Ann,

Got your message. I thank you and your Bible study for all your prayers. It's nice to know people I don't even know are praying for me. What a world! What a God! I must say I am disappointed with going through chemo again but if I have to, I will and I am. I'm not giving up; that's too much wasted energy. I have things to do yet. You know, Ann, my silence is easier for me to deal with when it comes to my thoughts and feelings. I have a fear of saying the wrong things because I used to lash out with words I truly never meant. I was mean, I know, and didn't know how to say I'm sorry. No one ever said they were sorry to me when they did me wrong, so I just always thought that was the way of life, and I thought life sucked. Sometimes, a lot of times, we learn that life is really nice with all the ups and downs. And, then, when we change, people don't believe it because I was wrong more often than right. I can understand where they're coming from. No one ever told me they loved me other than my husband and my kids. It was hard for me to say "I love you" to my kids. It seemed like only words. I thought taking care of my family with my little so-called knowledge, was the way to say I love them. I didn't know words enhanced our feelings. If someone did me wrong, I thought, well, they don't like me and visa-versa. Going to church these past few years taught me things or just opened my eyes.

I learned so much, but it seems too late, because scars are scars and not easily erased, nor do memories get erased. Like the fight I had with you when you were fifteen or sixteen. I had to be out of my mind to fight with you. I was a crazy person, not even a mother! Did I ever tell you that I was sorry about it? Probably not, but I am now, and I am very, very sorry I hit you. Forgive me. I was nuts in plain English.

There are a lot of things I did wrong with all of my kids, and I have many regrets. But in my heart I asked God to forgive me, and I'm learning to forgive others and myself. I find I have more peace or something now than I've ever had before. I don't worry about things. I pray about them. If it weren't for you, I wouldn't be where I am now in my beliefs. I have years behind me that I could have done something about my believing in God, but on my own did nothing, until you. You gave me the inspiration, the wanting to know more about God and how much He truly loves us all. You showed me much and I'd need much more paper to go into small details that were a giant and wonderful fulfillment in my life.

Well, Ann, I knew there was a hidden secret about owning a computer. I could write a book to all my kids listing "I'm Sorry" forgive me for this or that. I do have many regrets, but I promise not to repeat them if ever the opportunity arises. I'm still learning about life; it feels good to learn. It makes life easier and so much nicer. Who knows, maybe I am really crazy after all!!! That'll be "OK" too.

Ann, I'm stopping, this was supposed to be a littttttle note. Let me know if it goes through. Love you more than words can say. As for my grandkids, loving them the way I do, there are not words. But I tell them I love them, those words to them come so easily.

Talk to you soon.

Love,

Mom

Ann's response to her mother's letter:

Dear Mom,

You just don't know how powerful and healing your words are to me. Thank you and I love you and I forgave you a long time ago.

I think when God came into my life; He began to do a great work in my heart that is still under construction ... thankfully. I did have a lot of pain in my life but when I started asking you and Dad about your childhoods ... well, neither of you really had a childhood. And, you Mom, especially, went through a type of hell that no one, especially a precious little girl, should ever have to go through. God only knows what hell your father must have suffered as a kid himself to grow up and be so twisted. And his mother must have suffered with deep, deep depression since that is the legacy she left with her own children.

It is NEVER too late to change, or grow, or heal with God. Nothing, but nothing is impossible with God. There is always HOPE and LOVE and FORGIVENESS with Him. And God wants this life for us to be good too, not just heaven; He is not a mean God, but a merciful Father.

I am sooooo proud of you, Mom. I know it is really hard and scary to look back sometimes. But God said that He wants to put truth in the innermost places of our lives and that includes the deepest recesses of our hearts ... God sees and knows but will not make us do anything. We have to ask for His help and then He cannot "not help us."

He has to help us because He cannot break His promises to us. And He wants to help us ... He is our perfect loving Father.

Thank you Mom for your love and your desire to allow God to heal you. You cannot imagine the power you have to turn bad into good. Love is the most powerful thing in this world. We know that because the Bible tells us that God is Love.

I love you,

ANN XXOO

Ann's Growth

I've tried to portray the wisdom and the growth in Ann, a growth that can only be caused by God as Ann presented more and more of herself to Him for healing. Yet, I still see her struggling with self-doubt and self-rejection at times. I know Our Lord will continue to teach Ann as she seeks His guidance.

Insights from Ann

"I still have old me trying to defend me, my worth, my place in life, my importance-me. I don't have to do that, and I don't do that as much as I used to. When Jeff (mostly it's with Jeff) is mean to me or irresponsible or immature or angry, I don't have to think badly and respond the same. I can overcome his evil with good and I don't even have to feel like being nice to Jeff to be nice to him. After I do the right thing, then I feel better but it's usually not while doing the right thing that I feel right. That's a mouth full.

But when I think of my mother's childhood and all that she went through I think she probably did the best she knew how to do."

I wish everyone could know Ann. When you meet her, you immediately see the openness and the eagerness of interaction available to you. But more important, you will be able to appreciate how God enables a child to develop coping skills that suffice for the child. Talking with Ann you will see her understanding of these coping mechanisms, her tendency to use them automatically and inappropriately as an adult and the importance of directing the energy behind them into positive behavior for today.

CHAPTER 9

No One Would Listen

It is interesting to recall how I perceived this young lady, who was one of my students at the Christian school. Annmarie appeared perfect in every way imaginable. Her physical beauty was obvious to everyone but her. That made her even more attractive. She had a smile that drew you in and wrapped you up in warm feelings. Kindness was the norm for Annmarie; artificial she was not.

Years later, when Annmarie came to my office seeking help for all the anxiety and pain she had held within all these years, I realized how well a child can mask what she is actually feeling. Annmarie had chosen coping mechanisms that were very good ones. They kept her very safe and were all legitimate attributes. But, she also kept much hidden from her friends, family and teachers.

Annmarie had developed great acting skills. She was in all the school plays and did wonderful mimes. The "performer" was ever-present. But as we began to work together, I realized that she had been acting in her day-to-day life as well. This was her only safety.

I can still see Annmarie strolling the halls, surrounded by her friends. If you saw her, your thoughts would be of seeing a very happy, attractive, and well-balanced young person enjoying her high-school years. Never would you think of a young person who was deeply hurting, riddled with guilt and running from memories that at times overwhelmed her. Her disguise was almost perfect, for she was one of the most-liked young people in her school, by both peers and staff.

As you will see, this young girl had a secret to keep. She had a need to run from much inside her head. The following story is of Annmarie as a little girl told by Annmarie as a big girl.

A Big Girl Tells A Little Girl's Story

I recently spoke with Annmarie who has decided to tell her horrifying story of molestation after sixteen years. She is speaking out on behalf of those children who have suffered in the past and relive their experiences through the new lives they now live. She also wants to send a message to those children today who are living secret lives with people they love and trust, and also hate because of the confusing pain they experience. The pain is confusing because as children they question whether the things that are happening are all part of growing up.

Annmarie's story begins when she was about nine years old. At least that's what age she thinks she was when her stepfather began to touch her in places that no one had touched her before. As a child this was a person who made life at home easier. Growing up without a father in the home was not easy for her. When the toilet was broken, the hot water heater broke, the living room needed to be painted, the grass needed to be mowed, or a Christmas tree had to be cut and put in the stand, her mother had neither the talent nor the time to complete such tasks. Having a man around to help was a relief for mother and daughter—until that man began to touch the daughter. Annmarie describes her state of mind as confused and scared. No one had ever spoken to her about this before. There weren't TV movies out about incest, and even if there were, she wouldn't have seen them because her Mother had taken their television away when Annmarie was about five years old. When the incest first began, Annmarie says she was confused because she didn't know if this was normal or not. As she got older—months older—she began to realize it wasn't right. If it were right, it wouldn't be done in secret. It wouldn't be done in a secluded basement, a dark attic, or under covers when her mother was around.

She was scared because someone who had brought good things to her home life was now bringing bad, secretive things, and she didn't know how to stop them. She says that she thought about telling someone. She felt like she would burst open, as when you take a pin to a balloon, if she didn't tell someone. She wanted to tell her mother, but thought that it would be her word against her stepfather's, and grown-ups always believe other grown-ups. After giving it much thought, she decided to confide in her closest friend at the time, Susan. One day after school, when no one was home, Annmarie and Susan sat with their clothes on in an empty bath tub with the glass doors closed and the bathroom door closed. Annmarie revealed her secret to her friend, hoping for answers and help. She got neither. Susan had listened to Annmarie's pain and sworn herself to secrecy. The molestation continued. Most instances occurred when Annmarie's mother was at church meetings and her stepfather was watching Annmarie and her brother.

I asked Annmarie why she is telling her story now, after sixteen years of living with the pain of her abusive childhood. Annmarie stated, "When I look at my beautiful, pure, innocent, seven-month-old daughter, I think back to my own childhood and wonder how my mother looked at me. Did she feel the same need to protect me from anything painful? And if she did, I ask myself, where did she fail? When I figure out where she failed, I will do whatever it takes to protect Anna from any form of the pain I feel each time I look at her." Annmarie also noted that she sometimes wonders if she is a little bit jealous of Anna's purity now and the purity she will continue to experience provided she is protected. Does Annmarie wish her mother had been as conscientious as she is now?

Annmarie said that she resents her mother for going out so much. There were weeks when her mother was out four or five nights a week. While her mother was trying to help herself experience healing from the painful childhood she lived through (alcoholic father, living with her grandmother in her house since the family couldn't afford their own home), she was indirectly afflicting pain on her daughter. Pain, that years later, Annmarie would struggle to be healed from. So, you may say to yourself, "a lot of mothers go out often and trust their live-in boyfriend to watch their children. How can Annmarie place all that blame on her mother and say she failed?"

Annmarie painfully admits, "She failed to listen and believe me when I was finally brave enough to speak out." It had taken all she had to walk down the stairs to her mother in the living room on a night when Ralph was not home and Annmarie was supposed to be in bed. In her baby doll pajamas, Annmarie told her mother that Ralph was touching her in places she didn't think he should. Annmarie says that she does not remember her mother's response. She feels that she did not believe her, but said she would speak to Ralph. Annmarie also does not think that things stopped then—possibly temporarily— but began again. The one thing she does remember is a feeling of anger that her mother didn't believe her and demand that Ralph leave the house immediately. "After all," Annmarie says, "didn't my mother want to protect me from anything that was possibly hurting me?" She feels that from that time on she always has felt that her mother loved Ralph more than her. Annmarie is angry that her mother indirectly allowed the sexual abuse to occur and then when her mother was aware of it did not stop it. One of the most difficult times that Annmarie remembers in terms of trust being broken involved a break of secrecy. Susan, who was a non-Christian neighborhood friend, had been a bad influence on Annmarie. She had gotten her involved with smoking, stealing money from her mother, buying "rock magazines." and shoplifting (once!) She was older than Annmarie was, and they had gotten to be friends from the neighborhood. Annmarie's mother must have become a Christian when Annmarie was nine years old, because when Annmarie was about to enter fifth grade in the Jefferson Grammar School, her mother decided she would go to the church school. Annmarie describes the day her mother took her out of that school. Annmarie and her mother walked down Washington Avenue on that warm summer day. Annmarie had tears in her eyes when she thought about her new crossing guard orange sash that had never been used. She describes her anger that this was happening to her. She had friends and a routine and had to leave both to start to make new friends and a new routine. She couldn't believe her mother was doing this to her. They have talked, fought and cried about the change. Her mother said if Annmarie didn't like it after several months she could leave. That never came to be the case. When Annmarie began the new school, she tried to stay in touch with her friends, but it was difficult. She says she grew apart from Susan. Annmarie remembers getting into an argument with Susan, and the threat that came back to Annmarie was "If you don't, I'll tell everyone what Ralph did to you." Annmarie describes the feeling of horror that came upon her. At that time she had not told her mother or anyone else. Fear and anger gripped her. Annmarie does not remember what Susan wanted but can still recall the intense fear of this long kept secret being revealed. Susan made new friends, and Annmarie believes she probably told them, but does not know for sure since the time that Annmarie told Susan, she told three other people—her mother, her husband, her friend, Maggie and now four—her counselor and friend, Mrs. Mog.

The birth of Annmarie's first child brought forth much of the emotional trauma, anxiety and pain that she had hidden far below the surface of the conscious mind.

When she came for counseling, she consciously began to process the terrible wrong that had been committed against her.

During the most difficult period of a person's life, adolescence, Annmarie lived with guilt. The guilt was a result of a young girl's belief that she should somehow protect her stepfather's grandchildren from him. She knew that he often babysat for them and felt that they were not safe. How does a young girl get any help? There was none available for her when she was a child, even when she reached out for it. So, when in Annmarie's senior year of high school, her young nieces told their dad that their grandfather was hurting them, he was arrested and was eventually sent to prison. Annmarie filled with self-blame and guilt. She felt that if she had done something, her stepfather would not have been able to abuse his young granddaughters.

Annmarie found that she could not keep her house the way she would like it; she had a hard time throwing things out, and she often was engulfed with feelings of anxiety and depression. Obsessive-Compulsive Disorder traits such as collecting things helped her block out the emotional memories that she had repressed. Such persons can fixate on needing to save all the paper items that come into the home; they rationalize that they may one day need the information or the coupons. Before long they have containers full of junk mail but the necessity to keep it persists. Thoughts about the papers of future importance take up the space in the brain that might want to dwell on the unpleasant past. Annmarie's compulsion to save every piece of paper and her obsessive belief that she could not keep house kept all the "ugly" away, but they also made it difficult for her to be the mother and wife she wanted to be.

Annmarie is blessed with a wonderful husband who has been instrumental in her healing. Her faith in a loving God is very much intact as she gives of herself and her talents to her church. And because she had such a need to stay away from the pain as a child, she developed great abilities in the things she loved, such as acting. She strove to put her whole mind and soul into these activities, allowing no space or time for the unpleasant.

This wonderful and brave young mother and wife will continue to heal even though it will be a difficult journey. She will be on the alert for her young children, striving always to provide them with love and safety. It will take time, and she will need the help of others, but God will return to her the years the locusts have eaten away.

CHAPTER 10

The Girl with No Head

As a Christian counselor, I have developed the deepest respect and love for adults who have survived extremely difficult childhoods. And one of the things I marvel at is the creative manner in which they accomplished this. I previously noted in this book that God certainly does provide a way of escape, as His Word reminds us.

Cynthia came to see me as a young woman who was going places in the corporate world. She was happily married to a young man who was also in the corporate scene but in another area of expertise. To this day, I cannot clearly tell you what her presenting problem was. As I remember, she often felt sad and disoriented, with bouts of anger that she could not understand.

I can still see her walking into my office offering me her hand as she introduced herself. She took a seat on the very end of the office sofa with an air of confidence, not at all as someone having a difficult time. I loved her mind. I found myself smiling and often laughing aloud at her quick wit.

When I do the Safe Room Technique with this young woman, who is now a mother herself, she sees several children of various ages in her room. There is the "bad girl," (she has a mean look on her face) along with those who are "jumping rope" (they seem to be having great fun) and "those who hide." She sees a desperate eleven-year-old, taking off her head and laying it in the back seat of her father's car.

Cynthia is the girl I referred to in the chapter about "hiding." She was sexually abused as a child and at the age of eleven, decided to put everything bad that was happening to her into her head and then take her head off so she would not have to deal with it. Now, wasn't that clever?

This young girl had already used other avoidance methods such as trying to play and keep busy, but sexual abuse often makes this difficult. This is especially true when the abuse happens in your home, where you are supposed to be the safest. Small children have no way of knowing that this is not supposed to happen, they just know that it scares them, hurts them, confuses them and causes them to fragment into many avenues of escape. Cynthia's mother used to say that she seemed unaware of her actions, as if she "didn't have a head on her shoulders." This became an out for the very clever child.

When this child was in the first grade, she desperately wanted help. Her fear and frustration were so great that she began to act out in school. Do you know how far that got her? She was labeled a "bad girl" and the cause of a perfectly good teacher's resignation. Didn't anyone think that perhaps this child needed help? Poorly behaved children bother us and hurt our egos. We think we should be able to parent correctly, teach correctly, and in turn they will be good. I was proud of this child's tenacious spirit. It was also about this time that the child learned that she was adopted and began to use that as a reason for the abusive treatment she was receiving. After all, no one really wanted her. Perhaps this is why one who was supposed to look out for her betrayed her.

She was a bright child and finally learned that no one was going to help if she were completely out of hand. So she "got better." Oh my, I wish she had gotten help. But, how are we to know? As a teacher, I was not trained to view such behavior as a cry for help. Now, more and more teachers are getting this insight. But, it takes a brave teacher with the administration's support to say, "Let's find out what is bothering this child." Let's hope that in Christian schools, we always ask for God's help.

At the age of twelve, she began to cry when she was being molested; the perpetrator now knew that she was no longer dissociating. In prior instances, she looked off into space and allowed him to do what he wanted. Largely due to her age, the pain and humiliation was so great that she couldn't take her head off fast enough; she couldn't get up in the sky fast enough (One of the ways that she dissociated was to float above herself). Realizing this, he promised not to do it anymore, but warned her never to tell. It must be their secret. After all these years of blaming herself, as kids do, she had no intention of telling. Now that it was over, why would she ever want to let anyone know? It will take her two years from that time to completely repress the memory.

Now, what does a young girl do with all of that anger? She gets even, of course. How does she do that? She releases her anger by ruining her own life, she doesn't want her parents to think for one minute that they did a good job of raising her. So, her schoolwork suffers and she becomes promiscuous.

At age fourteen, she found herself pregnant and in an abortion clinic. Oh, how very difficult. The abortion did not go well, and the young teenager found herself bleeding profusely and in need of help. Her mother found her on the bathroom floor and took her to the emergency room. From her bed she heard the doctor say to her mom that thirty minutes later in getting help and she would have died. What did Cynthia's mother say to her once the crisis had passed? She said nothing—absolutely nothing. She did not yell at her for not coming to her so she could be there for her. And, she didn't even get angry at her for bringing this form of disgrace into the family. Consequently, when this young woman and I walk down the hallway in her safe room visualization, we come upon the door created by the fourteen-year-old. Behind this door hangs a sign that reads,

"Live Recklessly; Who Cares?" This room reveals the awful truth she feels inside: "No one cares."

The fourteen-year-old at the hospital, after having the abortion and almost dying, dons a black leather jacket as she gets up from the table. She is going to need the "toughness" that goes along with that jacket and the strength that comes with such a fragment. Doesn't it make us think about how often we judge such teenagers without thinking that most likely they are just finding a way to cope with a very difficult situation? So often I have heard these kids say, "I don't need anyone. I can take care of myself. If they think I care, they are mistaken. And, no one better get in my way."

Cynthia's promiscuous behavior continued, but at this juncture she had been successful in repressing the memories of the sexual abuse. Thus, she left room for the intelligent one to make herself a viable part of her life. She did not do well in high school, but in college she excelled and eventually earned her Master's degree.

Cynthia and I have talked frequently about how the religious part of her is amazed at the not-so-godly attitude of other parts. But it makes sense: All fragments have yet to make Him Lord of their lives. Some of them may feel that He wasn't there for them; this results in inner resistance. Again, we understand the importance of David's statement in Psalm 51:6: "Behold, You desire truth in the innermost parts, And in the hidden part You will make me to know wisdom." Just how much of ourselves do we hide from God, not allowing Him to give to us the wisdom we so long for and need? Again, the inability to lead a stable Christian life may indicate that we have hidden a part of ourselves from God. Bouts of depression, sadness, lack of self-control, low self-esteem, poor interpersonal relationship skills and anger also indicate hidden parts. As Christians, we may reject the notion that we can hide parts of ourselves from God. Rather than address these things that cause negativity in our Christian experience, we make such comments as, "I'm not perfect." One cannot argue with that statement, but Jesus is very explicit in wanting us to strive for perfection as He states in John 5:48. Becoming more God-like affords us greater safety in this life.

Another of Cynthia's fragments is the "angry one." She seems to have a will of her own and often does not submit to God at all. She rants and raves, abandoning herself totally to the force behind the anger. Again, how was a child who was abused sexually from age two to twelve to survive? Allowing anger to arise makes us feel more powerful. Without a doubt, the neighborhood bully always has a frightened child that is constantly overshadowed and held down by the "bully" part of him or herself.

Part of the Safe Room technique has the client visualize doors behind which lie the reasons for a particular emotional fragment, such as fear or anger. When I did this with Cynthia, she saw places where a relative who should have protected her actually sexually molested her. Because Cynthia was once again pregnant, we felt it best not to continue this disturbing work until after the baby was born.

Cynthia had twin boys and was very busy with her three sons. I did not see her for a while. But one day she went to visit the relative who had molested her. When the relative wanted to hold her child, she began to panic and did everything she could do to keep from running from the house. When Cynthia and I continued our memory work it was clear why she had such an overwhelming fear of the relative.

Cynthia has made wonderful progress. It has not been an easy journey for her. She has confronted the relative, who is quite elderly now, and she is seeking God's help in allowing her fragments to work as a whole.

Cynthia and I have learned how much the child blames herself for everything and how large a part self-rejection plays in our lives. This calls to mind Jesus commanding his disciples to love others as they love themselves. Jesus also told them to love one another as the Father in Heaven loves them. Obviously, Jesus wanted us to be aware that we might not love ourselves as we should, but loving ourselves can only come in knowing how precious we are to God. Have we thought about that wonderful harvest that is there to be gathered? As "Pastor," "Deacon," "Sunday School teacher," "Choir Member," "Good Church Member," we often ignore the hurting children within ourselves and hide them behind the important roles we play in our Christian communities. The children within ourselves never have an opportunity to experience God's love for them—a love that is constant and not based on what we do for Him. Those fragments within Christian adults often work double-time to feel loved by God. How very sad it is if God's love is viewed as something that must be earned or worked for. The child within us needs to know that God's love was set in place before time and will not change. He does not love us more because we obey Him, even though obedience is our way of expressing our love to Him and provides for us a safe lifestyle. And we cannot cause Him to love us less by refusing to obey Him. Our negative behavior only makes this life more difficult for us.

Of course, Cynthia chose many self-destructive avenues in attempts to squelch the negative thoughts inside her—as a means to quiet all the arguments inside her head. Doing so left her with much self-loathing that had to be addressed and continues to be addressed.

CHAPTER 11

Only God

A young woman wrote to me this morning; I could hear the agony in her email. She had inadvertently found a picture that her husband had downloaded from a pornography website. They had a small son and their lives had been going well. Now, what was she to do? She told him how awful he was, got him to a place where he lied and then to another spot where he gave a half-truth. Finally, she asked if he really expected her to believe that this was the only time he had ever done anything like that. In her mind and heart all their dreams were gone—their marriage was no longer something she could live in. So, why did she write to me? Obviously, she did not want things to end; she wanted someone to assure her that there was some sort of an answer.

This email came after my husband, Denny, and I had eaten in one of our favorite hangouts, McDonalds, where, as we ate a leisurely breakfast, we talked about the many serious things that were on my mind. That is something rather wonderful about my husband—He just lets me go on and on about what I am thinking and then tells me that I should write about it.

Today was a day when I was feeling so strongly the inability for us to understand the heart, actions and motives of another person. We might give understanding, but do we understand?

People who are hurting, who have pain, are often those who seek out God. They go to a church hoping that somehow this will be a place where they can be "real." A place where someone will see all that goes on inside of them—deep inside—and will accept and love them just the same. They hear of the love of God, make a commitment to follow in that love and then try so hard to give a "Christian life" to God. It seems the normal thing to do. After all, He loved them enough to die for them, so now it is their turn to give back, as though God had a need of something. They feel compelled to demonstrate to God that they are worthy of His love.

Throughout our lives we are taught that things must be earned. If we eat everything on our plates, we will get dessert. If we do well in our studies, we will get a good mark. And the list goes on of what we must do to earn those things we want. This indoctrination is not something one easily puts aside.

New Christians immediately put the "Christian" part of themselves on display. They come to all the services, volunteer for whatever job comes along, no matter how small or big, and strive to do whatever they think pleases God.

When I accepted Christ at the age of twelve, it was as if I was reaching for a lifeline. I had already tried to take my own life, and everything was dark and hopeless. The joy I felt being loved by Christ in all my misery was indescribable. In my mind there was nothing about me to love. Life had shown me that I was unlovable, and I had responded by drawing within myself. I couldn't look at people when I talked to them, and I rarely talked. My body seemed to be huge and awkward, which when I look back, was not the case at all. I was a pre-teen without a friend until Christ came into my life. How very fortunate I was, because I experienced that God loved all the "awfulness" that seemed to be me. I could not understand it, but I knew it to be the case. God loved me. I found that I quickly began to grow, both spiritually and emotionally. The world became a place in which I could survive and perhaps make a difference.

If you don't come to God under these circumstances, as a child with no hope, you might find yourself easily caught up in the trap of thinking that you need to be something for God. As we grow older, we have time to develop different ways to somehow give ourselves some significance. If we have musical ability, then surely that is something we have to offer. Maybe you are quite intelligent and have acquired a great deal of knowledge. Maybe you have a great sense of humor. So, we pull out all that we have "become" and shrink from much of what we feel we are within. We try to prove our worthiness to be called the children of God. And, I cannot help but wonder how big a part the Christian community plays in this.

Do we encourage new believers to begin at the beginning, like they are just babes in Christ and we—the body of believers—are there to love and encourage them? I wish this were always the case but feel that often this does not happen.

Too often, I believe, expediency leads us to place these "babes in Christ" in roles for which they are not yet sufficiently mature. When I talk with pastors and church people about newly converted people in positions of responsibility, they remind me that there just aren't enough people to do the job. That reminds me of when Jesus fed the five thousand. Until the disciples told Him that they did not have enough food, until they gave Him what food they could scrounge up, He was not free to do the miracle of feeding the five thousand with five loaves and two fishes. Shouldn't we in the church wait on God to provide? Can we present our need to Him and simply ask that He meet that need? What if we never get an opportunity to see such wonderful miracles, but, instead, throw our babes in Christ into the arena of sacrificial service even though they have yet to experience the reassurance of God's love for them just as they are? Why not lovingly bottle-feed these new Christians, share our growth with them and allow them to bask in God's love for them as they are? Then they will be free to delight in this love and give Him those things that lie within them that don't seem right—things they cannot understand but want to be gone from their lives. They can do this, because they have been shown the unconditional love of the Body of Christ, a love that requires nothing from them.

This allows them to feel safer, and this safety gives them the OK to become real. There is no longer a need to pretend or to try to be always acceptable to others or to God, because we have learned that we are already acceptable to Him and greatly loved just as we are.

I often feel in my personal life that I miss out on some wonderful blessings and provisions of God, because I am busy trying to do everything on my own. God taught me that when I do something, I get what Carol can do, but when I allow Him to provide and to do the work through me, I get what God can do. I wish I had never gone down the road of doing things on my own, but that is a technique that I learned well in childhood out of necessity. I can still remember many occasions between ages seven and thirteen, telling myself that I could do it, that I had to be able to do it. Even today, I continue to fall into the behaviors of the child until God pulls me up short. He reminds me of my need for His help. He reminds me that I am in His kitchen and trying to do what is His to do.

Several years ago, a wonderful Bible teacher called me at seven-thirty in the morning telling me that he needed my help; he needed some Bible verses that would give some insight into a problem he was having. I smiled inwardly because I was certainly aware that his knowledge of the scriptures far exceeded mine. He told me how his best friend had lost his seventeen-year-old daughter. She was standing in front of their home and a drunk driver ran into her and killed her. My friend had tried to comfort this dad; he had done everything he knew to do but was hoping that I had some scripture that might bring further solace and encouragement to his friend. I said to him, "I can't think of any scriptures, but a television commercial comes to my mind." My friend did not get upset nor did he hang up on me; he waited. I asked him if he remembered the Excedrin commercial where a mother and daughter were in the kitchen together and the daughter had an Excedrin headache and was saying to her mother, "Mother, please; I would rather do it myself." I shared with my friend that I thought he was in God's kitchen. Only God could console his friend and as long as he was trying so hard, his friend would continue to look toward him and not be left to God's comfort. He understood what I was saying, hung up and later told me that, indeed, when he got out of God's way, God was there for his friend.

Expectations of what we ought to be for others or what they should be for us can cause us some serious setbacks. It was wonderful to hear God tell me this past year that He didn't want me to have expectations of others or even of myself because He wanted to surprise me with His provision. My friend who was trying to help his friend had unrealistic expectations of himself, causing his friend to look to him for the help that only God could provide.

Back to the young woman who emailed me this morning. Without a doubt, her husband's behavior had to be disappointing. But she also felt caught off-guard, out of control, helpless.

When I answered this young wife and mother, I reminded her of all the pain that her husband's behavior would bring to mind—all the negative emotions and fears that would well up inside her, almost as though she would surely drown, suffocate. You see, this young woman and her sisters were victims. Others who should have protected them had used their young bodies for child pornography.

I also chose this critical time to remind her of behaviors that she has had in the past and still is besieged with at times that do not make sense to her—anger, withdrawal, and negativity. Perhaps her husband also was dealing with something in the innermost part of his being that caused this particular negative behavior. Please understand that I am not condoning his behavior. Instead I hope you will take just a moment to think of behaviors that you cannot condone in yourself, and open your mind to what I am about to say.

Only God can truly understand our hearts. In 1 John 3:19, 20 it reads: *"This is how we know that we belong to the truth, and how we set our hearts at rest in his presence whenever our hearts condemn us. For God is greater than our hearts, and he knows everything."*

That which we can do as God's children is to give grace to ourselves first and ask His help in seeing into the innermost parts. There we will find the source of negative coping mechanisms that harm our lives and perhaps the lives of those we love. When we do this, we will find that grace abounds in our lives. No longer will others' behaviors affect the manner in which we want to behave.

More and more, God has enabled me to understand the origin of some of the feelings I struggle with. I believe that in making myself vulnerable, I may somehow help those who read this to understand.

Today in my Christian calendar, I read what was written for January. The author talked about evidence that Jesus liked to have fun. He wondered how Christians got the idea that a "good" Christian is a solemn Christian.

I don't think that most of my friends see me as a solemn Christian or even as one who does not know how to have fun. But I struggle with this on the inside. You see, this is not a reference point for me; I saw no one having fun when I was a child. A long or angry face was the norm. Anger and misery at those times of the year that should have been the happiest were what I came to expect. Even in her later years after having accepted Christ, my mother talked about how much she hated the holidays. Growing up, my sister and I went next door and watched the neighbors open their many Christmas gifts because we did not receive gifts. The only positive thing at our home was the aroma of Christmas dinner. My mother was a good cook and seemed to enjoying cooking. Now, I admit that I enjoyed the food but not the time spent at the table eating. We always waited for some sort of sarcastic remark from our stepfather. I can still see my brother's face almost in his plate as he shoveled the food into his mouth and then quickly left the table.

Pure joy—happiness—glad-to-be alive were not emotions that I ever experienced as a child. So, I am aware of the sad child within who leans so heavily on Jesus. Yet, because I am aware of her and why she exists, she does not control my life and my behavior. But, in all honesty, she is wary of good things coming her way even though her Heavenly Father continues to send them daily. He understands so well that "that which is crooked cannot be straightened," as Solomon says in the first chapter of Ecclesiastes. Fortunately, or miraculously, as the child puts her hand in Jesus' hand, she walks in His joy and the hope that lies in Him.

The child within an adult who has been mistreated has knowledge that is extremely important. She knows the need for joy in a child's life. She is a constant reminder of how God wishes to work through her and to provide for others' happiness and a "joie de vivre" that she never experienced in those around her. Because of her and all she knows, I don't ever have to say that I am not a morning person—and others best leave me alone. It is great to know that I can put aside negative feelings and listen to someone even when it is not "a good time" for me.

Oh, the lessons that the hurt and painful parts of one's self can teach us!

I know so well the courageous young women who shared their stories in this book. They wanted to do it and would have revealed their names if they knew that others would not be hurt. They chose different coping mechanisms that ended up controlling their lives. Yet, even though one coping mechanism seems to dominate, they all share a common repertoire, each ready to be used when needed. The coping mechanism of choice is often the one they saw exhibited the most or the one that helped the most.

As a child, no more than eight years of age, I thought that if I could do things right, be good and help everyone, maybe they wouldn't dislike having me around so much. That behavior is still a part of me and I must continually ask my Father not to allow that to keep me from being in the center of His will.

I am not saying that my mother's primary goal was to make me feel unwanted, because I know that she was dealing with difficult things in her own life. She married at fifteen and had her first child at seventeen. My father was killed in a car accident about three months before I was born. We were often told that she never wanted children. It was our father who wanted them. As an adult it is easy for me to understand all the unpleasantness she experienced when she was still only a child. Her parents raised eight children but did not know how to meet their emotional needs. So mother just passed her thoughts and frustrations on to us without knowing or caring how they might affect us. After all, she was surviving a difficult life.

So often we do this to the inner child. We try to make her take on the understanding of the adult without validating her feelings and acknowledging her misconceptions. We are busy repressing, pushing down into the innermost parts of ourselves that hurt and pain, hoping never to hear from it again. Unfortunately, that is not what happens.

When we get a cut on our finger, it sometimes gets infected. We watch as the wound scabs over. Every time we hit it against something, we again experience great discomfort. We need to apply peroxide or antibiotic cream before that scab forms again. The same is true of the unhealed child that we have buried beneath a "tough" outer emotional skin. When the pain of the child is evident, we can begin the healing process by embracing the child, rather than suppressing it. Then we can begin to experience wholeness; a greater sense of being in control and an absence of anxiety. If those in the Body of Christ could be there for us in our pain, instead of simply dismissing it with a few scriptures, they would have the wonderful experience of being used by God to help a person heal from a hurtful past.

Not everyone is going to like me; I am not going to please everyone. Knowing this has allowed the need to make others happy to be a positive in my life, not a negative.

If I were not aware of my inability to make others happy and the fact that it is not my job, I would, in all likelihood, enable them to take advantage of me. But, that does not necessarily make me a better person than someone who chooses to survive the pain of the child by using anger or withdrawing as a means of coping. Often the people-pleaser seems to be so much better than someone who is coping through isolation or, at times, through anger. Using one coping mechanism rather than another in order to hide the pain of the child is not more helpful, in the long run, to the well-being of the person.

Twice in my counseling career, I prayed fervently that a new client of mine would find another counselor. What was it about these two people that frightened me? It was their one-dimensional anger. I did not know how to get past their anger to find the person it was protecting. And, to be honest, I didn't even want God to help me find the way; I just wanted to get away from them.

This was not God's plan, and, as I worked with these two people, I soon learned why they needed the anger. The more I accepted and validated the anger, the less angry they became and the more I enjoyed working with them. To this day, one is a close friend and the other has gone home to be with Jesus as she was terminally ill when she first came to me. She was able to lay her anger at Jesus' feet and to experience His joy for her life in the time that she had left. Only God can renew our minds and hearts when we have such anger.

Yes, it is only God who can do this type of miracle. Sometimes we are called to love and to stand beside, but we can never change the heart or the mind; that is a God-thing.

This evening a woman emailed me and shared that she is spending a lot of time in the dark closet. She feels little, and the closet seems to be a safe place for her. This is a behavior that this well-educated person has experienced at other times in her life. When she was a young child, she needed to hide in the closet where she would not hear the loud fighting between her parents. Her mother recently had to be put into a nursing home, and she is trying to cope without her. She is trying to cope with being alone and seemingly without a purpose. No one would know that she is having such difficulty, because she continues to go to her very responsible job and do many other things such as singing in the choir. But when she gets home, she often hides like she did as a child.

I realize that I cannot make the scary feelings go away. That is a job for God and this person. But, I can be there for her as she makes this journey. I am confident that God will bring her through this, but the frightened child will always be a part and will one day cause her to emerge from her hiding place. Her acceptance of this fear will prevent its being an isolation that pulls her into itself. Instead, she will be able to reason with it. The shutting aside of such fears allows them to hold a place in our emotions, ready to surface and take over our whole being when circumstances overwhelm us. It seems to me that often we try to push away our feelings without ever acknowledging their source. We do this so that we might be the person we have found to be acceptable.

Paul wrote that he was going to become all things to all men that he might save some. So often, we expect people to change so that they meet our expectations. We say they should be as we think they should be. Paul does not seem to have this attitude. Perhaps he would crawl into the closet with this hurting person and minister to her where she was. I can see Paul allowing someone to express her anger and genuinely wanting to help her find out why she believes she needs it.

I think that should be a goal for all of us—to ask the Father's help in walking with someone in their shoes and accepting their difficult behaviors as coping mechanisms. And even though the behaviors may be negative, we do not have to reject the person because of them. Perhaps we can be a means by which they can become "real" and able to present these parts of them to the Father for renewal.

Even more important, before we can be there for others, we must be there for ourselves. We must accept the small pockets of fear, anger, insecurity and inadequacy that we have pushed aside for so long and allow them to exist and to heal — allow them to be exposed to the whole of ourselves.

It is my hope that readers who relate to this book will give themselves an opportunity to heal from past hurts. That they will not reject themselves because of negative behaviors that they don't understand but rather will get the help they need to understand the source of those behaviors.

I like to refer to this process as the gathering of one's self. I love the scriptures found in Matthew 18, where Jesus talks about the children coming unto Him. Let us gather and give all of us to Jesus.

If you are reading this book but have not suffered the pain of these women, hopefully you will want to be a loving and accepting friend to someone who is in the process of healing.